THE END OF COLONIAL RULE IN WEST AFRICA

By the same author

A Life of Sir Samuel Lewis
Prelude to the Partition of West Africa
West Africa: the Former French States
France and West Africa (*editor*)
Nations and Empires (*co-editor with R. C. Bridges, Paul Dukes and William Scott*)
West Africa Partitioned: Vol. 1, The Loaded Pause, 1885–1889

THE END OF COLONIAL RULE IN WEST AFRICA

Essays in Contemporary History

John D. Hargreaves

BOOKS
10 East 53d St., New York 10022
(a division of Harper & Row Publishers, Inc.)

© John D. Hargreaves 1979

All rights reserved. No part of this publication may be reproduced or transmitted, in any form or by any means, without permission

First published 1979 by
THE MACMILLAN PRESS LTD
London and Basingstoke

Published in the U.S.A. 1979 by
HARPER & ROW PUBLISHERS, INC.
BARNES & NOBLE IMPORT DIVISION

Printed in Great Britain

Library of Congress Cataloging in Publication Data

Hargreaves, John D.
    The end of colonial rule in West Africa.

    The first essay was published separately in 1976 under title: The end of colonial rule in West Africa.
    Includes bibliographical references and index.
    1. Africa, West—Politics and government—Addresses, essays, lectures. 2. Nationalism—Africa, West—Addresses, essays, lectures. I. Title.
DT476.2.H362 1979   966   79-12129
ISBN 0-06-492705-9

For Sheila, who lived through it too

Contents

Preface	ix
Acknowledgements	xv
Abbreviations	xvi

PART I. CHANGING PERSPECTIVES   1

1 Decolonization or Liberation?   3
   International pressures and the impact of the depression
   Effects of the Second World War
   The sudden death of West African colonialism

2 Wartime Origins of Political Transfer   24
   Native administration and political development
   Governor Burns, the Colonial Office and the Gold Coast Constitution
   The Labour government in the post-war world

3 Approaches to Decolonization in Sierra Leone   49
   The rejection of the Creoles
   The rise of the Youth League
   The aborting of "Stage One"
   The first decolonizers

4 Resisters, Collaborators, Heritors   70
   After-thoughts on "African nationalism"
   The triumph of the CPP and its rural base
   Politicians, chiefs and peasants: Variations on a theme
   Interim evaluations

PART II. SOME PROFESSORIAL FOOTNOTES 87

5 Changing Views from an Ivory Tower 89

6 The Idea of a Colonial University 99

7 History: African and Contemporary 112

Notes 123

Index 135

Preface

More than twenty years ago – for reasons in which chance now seems to have played a considerable part – I began a major study of the European partition of West Africa in the later nineteenth century. This has proved a much longer haul than I then expected; it is not finished yet. Working in a period of fierce but stimulating historiographical debate I have found the complexity of the evidence resistant to simplified explanations; those who know my work on this will not expect them here. I have very great sympathy for the distinguished former Prime Minister who defined the most serious problems he had had to deal with as "events", and I clearly do not accept the doctrine that *histoire événementielle* is somehow beneath intellectual contempt. The map of modern Africa owes much to such apparent accidents as the impulses of temperamental individuals, or tangential contingencies arising from the internal politics of Europe. But the real challenge to a historian is to show how such random happenings interacted with underlying patterns of economic, social and psychological change and continuity; hence I have increasingly tried to set the dramatic events of 1885–1900 within a broader context of Afro-European relations, extending both backwards and forwards in time.

In 1963, relationships during the 1860s and 1870s were examined in *Prelude to the Partition of West Africa*. The general argument of that book, though I would present it somewhat differently now, still seems broadly acceptable. Europeans, notably the British, were endeavouring to draw independent West African states into the international economy by injecting the transforming forces of Christianity, civilization and commerce. British, and to a lesser degree French, sea power supervised a developing complex of commercial, cultural and political relationships which linked the fortunes of substantial minorities in both continents. Despite the hostile reactions induced by a name which in Hitlerite Europe had been associated with a very bad dog, these can be regarded as a system of "collaboration", in which African rulers, traders and *evolués* often willingly accepted the goals which Europeans claimed to be pursuing. By the 1880s, as *West Africa Partitioned* is in process of showing, the European partners were becoming more exacting. New demands (which may be directly or indirectly traceable to the increasing strains of international competition during a period of erratically interrupted capitalist growth) alienated these African elites and jeopardized the collaborative arrangements which had been established. Europeans extended formal political control, at first cautiously and reluctantly, increasingly with enthusiasm and vigour. By the 1890s West Africa had become a theatre of interest to organized imperialist movements, which sometimes brought decisive influence to bear on both the internal politics and the international relations of the major European states. Under these new pressures the peoples of West Africa passed, almost without exception, under formal colonial rule.

It is clearly neither possible nor desirable to write the history of European imperialism without placing a dominant emphasis on the changing behaviour of Europeans, for it was they who increasingly held the power to determine relationships. But nor could a historian, working sometimes in Africa but always in an environment sympathetic to the rediscovery of African history, regard African behaviour as uninteresting or irrelevant, as his "imperial" predecessors had often tended to do. It was not necessary to devise a "peripheral theory" of imperialism to realize that reactions or initiatives by African rulers or traders could affect the nature of the new relationships even more strongly than the intentions of Europeans. Nor did it seem sufficient to follow two distinguished Africanists in drawing simple distinctions between Africans who sought to maintain new forms of collaboration and those who turned to resistance, still less to accept their judgement that the former group were necessarily more forward-looking than the latter. Closer study showed that "collaborators" and "resisters" were often the same men, adapting their behaviour to changed perceptions of European intentions: understanding the complexities of their decisions could do much to explain the nature of the new colonial relationships.

In 1969 Terence Ranger and I, when invited to contribute to a collaborative work on colonialism in Africa, independently decided to devote much of our space to establishing this simple point.[1] Meanwhile, in a paper published in 1972, Ronald Robinson was giving a still wider and more provocative interpretation to the concept of collaboration which he had done so much to promote. Analysis of the strength and weakness of systems of Afro-European collaboration, Robinson now argued, could explain not only the establishment of colonial rule, but its continuance and its ultimate decline. Many of the old relationships which Europeans had established with African rulers or elites survived the shock of conquest; the new colonial governments, lacking the resources or the will to rule as tyrants, had to undertake a "reconstruction of collaboration", reforming some old alliances and creating new ones. Their chief weapon in doing so was the patronage of the colonial state – "the perquisites of office, honours, contracts, social services and all the favours that could be given or taken away through its administrative, land, fiscal and education policies"[2] – and these proved sufficient until after the Second World War.

The general effect of the closely focused studies of the colonial period which are now appearing is to confirm this emphasis on underlying continuities. Many African scholars are sceptical about the capacity of foreign rulers to bring about those economic, social and cultural transformations of which imperial ideologies had boasted; they emphasize the capacity of African institutions, culture and values to survive the changes in superstructure. Others are most impressed by the continuities in West Africa's economic relationships with Europe and the capitalist world economy, and may be less inclined to play down the capacity of colonial government to influence the long-term course of their development. In either case the colonial period becomes a phase in Afro-European relationships, rather than a distinct era; its end, like its beginning, has to be placed in a long historical context. Hence a historian who has lived and worked through the terminal years of colonial rule finds himself facing both the problems which E. H. Carr regards as the criteria of historical objectivity: how to recognize and attempt to transcend his own marginal involvement in the historical situation, how to see past sequences of partition, colonial rule and transfer of power in relation to the present and the future.

Both analogies and continuities between the beginning and the end of colonial rule are suggested in the essays which follow. In the 1930s and 1940s as in the 1880s and 1890s the context for changes in Afro-European relations seems to have been set by movements on a wider historical scene: by the international depression, the shifts of power in the world during the Second World War, the economic and political constraints upon both British and French empires which followed it. The effects, experienced not only in London and Paris but in colonial capitals where African resistance began to seem an increasing danger, made it necessary to undertake one more "reconstruction of collaboration", to move back from a formal relationship of dominance towards systems which implied political equality between freely contracting partners. And – though here the long-term consequences remain most obscure – the policies and ideologies of colonial imperialism began to be replaced by the new conventional wisdom of "partnership for development". It is no longer Christianity, civilization and commerce but social engineering, technical assistance and capital investment which are expected to harmonize the interests of Africa and Europe.

A final analogy reflects this historian's fear of theoretical oversimplification: there again seems to have been much indeterminacy about the detailed course of historical change. "Events" and individuals affected the course of history, at least in the short run (and, as Churchill once put it, it is always being affected by something or other). In 1875 the maintenance of British influence in the Gambia seems to have hinged upon Mr Samuel Plimsoll's indignation over maritime safety, rather than on any fundamental characteristic of British imperialism;[3] similarly, chance and the free decisions of individuals seem to have done as much as profound historical forces to determine that in 1978 the tiny Gambian Republic should provide Africa's best-working example of Western-style political democracy. Colleagues with more orderly minds find it disturbing that historical study should lead to such sceptical conclusions. To those who carry great or small responsibilities however it may suggest that the decisions they take can make a difference, though within limits much narrower than vain men imagine.

The first of these essays is basically the text of a pamphlet in which in 1976 I tried to present alternative explanations of the end of colonial rule to non-specialist readers with interests in contemporary history. Versions of conference papers follow, revised with the benefit of lively discussions with colleagues in Paris in 1976 and at Bellagio in 1977; both are modest but I hope reasonably substantial attempts to use the archival evidence now becoming available to illustrate some of the thinking (or absence of thinking) behind the detailed evolution of British policy. The fourth essay is new, an attempt to redress the Eurocentric bias of its predecessors by considering the nature of African initiatives and successes during the period of transfer of power. I have no original research to contribute here; but the extensive and interesting literature already available seemed to demand at least rudimentary discussion in the context of this volume. The three "professorial footnotes" are essentially attempts to assess my own marginal involvement, from within the British academic community, in the events I have described. Despite the occasional confessional note they are not undertaken in the spirit of *mea culpa*, but in the belief that such self-examination can help in the formation of objective judgements upon contentious events of the recent past.

Banchory, July 1978 JOHN D. HARGREAVES

Acknowledgements

For permission to reprint Chapter 1 I am grateful to the Historical Association: substantially it appeared as No G88 in their General Series. Chapter 2 was originally drafted in a different form for the Conference on the Transfer of Power in Africa, organized at Bellagio in September 1977 by Prosser Gifford and Roger Louis; the original version will appear in the volume which they are editing. Chapter 3 was originally prepared for an Anglo-French Colloquium on "Independence and Dependence: the relations of Britain and France with their former Territories", held in Paris in May 1976; the original version appears in *Decolonisation and After: the British and French Experience*, edited by W. H. Morris-Jones and George Fischer. I am grateful to the editors, and to the publishers, Frank Cass, for permission to reprint this material. Chapter 6 is reprinted from *African Affairs*, 72, 1973, by kind permission of the editors. Chapter 7 was a Presidential Address to the African Studies Association (UK) delivered in September 1973; it appeared in *African Research and Documentation*, 3, 1973, and is reproduced by permission of the editor.

I am grateful to Mrs Karen Stephen, Miss Freda Booth and Miss Catherine Hargreaves for their help in preparing the manuscript for publication.

Less formal but no less important debts of gratitude are owed to a very large number of friends and colleagues whose writings, comments on drafts, and conversation are largely responsible for such signs of coherence as may be detected in these essays. I will not attempt to name them all; but I must record with gratitude that two of these papers were first aired in the Aberdeen University African Studies Group and that all of them owe much to the shrewd criticism, often renewed at successive stages of composition, of Roy Bridges.

Abbreviations

APC	All Peoples' Congress (Sierra Leone)
AOF	Afrique occidentale française
CD & W	Colonial Development and Welfare
CO	Colonial Office
CPP	Convention Peoples' Party (Ghana)
FBC	Fourah Bay College (Sierra Leone)
FCB	Fabian Colonial Bureau
FIDES	Fonds d'investissement pour le Développment Economique et Social des Territoires d'Outre-mer
LSE	London School of Economics
NAs	Native Authorities
NAPD	*Native Administration and Political Development in British Tropical Africa.* Report by Lord Hailey, 1940–42 (Colonial Office, Confidential)
NCNC	National Council of Nigeria and Cameroons
NPC	Northern Peoples' Congress (Nigeria)
PAIGC	Partido Africano da Independencia da Guiné e Cabo Verde
PDG	Parti Démocratique de Guinée
PP	Parliamentary Papers
RDA	Rassemblement Democratique Africain
SLPP	Sierra Leone Peoples' Party
UPC	Union des Populations du Cameroun
WAFTU	West African Federation of Trade Unions
WFTU	World Federation of Trade Unions

Part I
Changing Perspectives

1 Decolonization or Liberation?

The term "decolonization" appears to have been coined in 1932 by M. J. Bonn, a German scholar who later migrated to the London School of Economics; but it did not pass into very general currency until two decades later.[1] During the inter-war period it was in the British Empire in Asia that such a process could most easily be discerned. In India, British governments between the wars were continually engaged in often stormy dialogue with the leaders of the Congress Party and the Muslim League over the manner and the timing of progress towards that Dominion status which as early as 1917 had been acknowledged as the goal of British policy; in 1928 the Donoughmore Commission's complex proposals set Ceylon well on the road to full responsible government. Increasingly the official historiography of the period taught that it was the purpose and destiny of the British Empire to liquidate itself by creating modernized societies ripe for independence in the modern world. This view received a classic exposition in the House of Commons (7 December 1938) from the Colonial Secretary, Malcolm MacDonald:

> The great purpose of the British Empire is the gradual spread of freedom among all His Majesty's subjects in whatever part of the world they live. That spread of freedom is a slow, evolutionary, process. In some countries it is more rapid than in others. In some parts of the Empire, in the Dominions, that evolutionary process has been completed, it is finished. Inside the Colonial Empire the evolutionary process is going on all the time. In some colonies like Ceylon the gaining of freedom has already gone very far. In others it is necessarily a much slower process. It may take generations, or even centuries, for the peoples in some parts of the Colonial Empire to achieve self-government. But it is a major part of our policy, even among the most backward peoples of

Africa, to teach them and encourage them always to be able to stand a little more on their own feet.

African political leaders might have been forgiven for receiving MacDonald's statement sceptically. In the Union of South Africa the completion of the evolutionary process towards Dominion status in 1910 had certainly not brought freedom to the African majority; and the stated aims of European settlers in Southern Rhodesia and Kenya suggested that the decolonization of Central and East Africa (might be directed along rather similar lines. As for West Africa, the passage of MacDonald's speech which most colonial administrators would have chosen to emphasize was the reference to "generations, or even centuries". Throughout the inter-war period it was normal for British officials to assume that the pace of paternalistic administration could not be forced by pressures for a transfer of political power. In a celebrated speech of 1920 Governor Hugh Clifford rejected the claims of elite politicians in the National Congress of British West Africa as "loose and gaseous talk";[2] this attitude was widespread, though not inconsistent with anxiety to exclude seditious influences from outside. Administrators who believed they had unlimited time in which to work could not plan towards decolonization, even if they accepted it (which not all seem to have done) as an ultimate objective.

Yet, strangely enough, MacDonald's historiographical perspective, his insistence on the self-liquidating character of British colonial rule, was widely accepted and endorsed by that very nationalist vanguard which Clifford derided. And indeed the colonial system proved capable of producing payments on account; even Clifford followed up his diatribe by actively pressing the Colonial Office to admit African elected members to the Legislative Councils.[3] So, as Professor Ayandele has recently argued, even the so-called radicals among the West African elite were in principle no less ready than the old conservative lawyers and doctors to collaborate with régimes to which they regarded themselves as heirs. In 1936 an unsuccessful prosecution for sedition made Nnamdi Azikiwe, editor of the Accra *African Morning Post*, a hero of nationalist militants; yet Zik's recent memoirs paint a nostalgically affectionate picture of Governor Hodson and other members of the "official tyranny" against which he was struggling.[4]

In France too, an official historiography looked forward to a liquidation of empire, though in a radically different form. When the *mission civilisatrice* was complete, France's African subjects would have become so culturally assimilated that they would think and behave like Frenchmen; and this would permit complete legal and political assimilation, with former subjects enjoying the same rights as Frenchmen within a Republic, one and indivisible. This magnificent dream had lost contact with reality during the imperial expansion of the later nineteenth century. Few Frenchmen seriously believed that millions of Africans could ever become assimilated in these ways; none would have tolerated a situation in which the assimilated millions held political power over Frenchmen. A new doctrine of "association" was evolved (which so far as Black Africa was concerned merely legitimized the authoritarian rule of the colonial bureaucracy); the rights of citizenship remained confined to a favoured elite – principally the residents of four old colonial towns in Senegal (Dakar, Gorée, Rufisque and Saint-Louis), plus some 2000 individual *évolués* who had earned the privilege by good behaviour under colonial rule.

Yet here too there was just sufficient substance in the decolonizing myth to win acceptance among its African beneficiaries. Leopold Sédar-Senghor, poet and philosopher, class-mate of Georges Pompidou, militant of the French Socialist Party and prisoner of the Germans in 1940, could be cited as living proof of the possibility of cultural assimilation and of its political consequences. And the Popular Front government of 1936 moved tentatively in directions which were more clearly signposted by de Gaulle's Brazzaville conference of colonial administrators in 1944 – towards a growing association of Africans with the conduct of public business within an indivisible French Union. Hence, when the future of France's African colonies was debated in the Second Constituent Assembly in September 1946, African Deputies concentrated their demands, not on independence, but on broader extensions of African political rights within the projected French Union. "There are no separatists on these benches," declared Félix Houphouët-Boigny, then regarded as a dangerously radical ally of the Communists. "There is only one possibility of emancipation for us, that is by remaining French," added Fily-Dabo Sissoko. "Do you mean that if men like Senghor . . . or myself are elected, non-Frenchmen would be coming here? Since when?" asked the Senegalese Socialist Lamine Guèye.[5] Faced as they were with settler offensives against the limited liberties which existed, these African Deputies had good tactical reasons for calling French Republicans to act in accordance with their own rhetoric. Yet, tactics apart, African leaders of this generation did usually take the official historiography of the *mission civilisatrice* pretty seriously.

The Second World War, as will be suggested later, changed many things; but it did not radically change the historical perspectives of the West African elite. Thus the all-African Committee on Constitutional Reform, which was appointed after the Gold Coast riots of 1948 had shaken British complacency, began its Report with an extended historical survey of "the relationship of the Gold Coast with Britain". Its central argument, borrowed from the British historian Martin Wight, was that the indigenous political traditions of Gold Coast Africans were wholly compatible with the promise of eventual self-government supposed to have been made in 1865.[6] And even when the *pace* of political change was accelerated, the basic notion of a *prepared* decolonization, a *constitutional progress* to self-government, remained generally acceptable to candidates for power. When in 1952 I first went to teach in Sierra Leone – a country with little recent experience of popular struggles – a topic of prime interest was how British constitutional experience could be applied to the process of decolonization which was at last gathering momentum. When, with youthful rashness, I agreed to give a series of extra-mural lectures on "Problems of Constitutional Development in West Africa", I was somewhat disconcerted to discover African members of both Executive and Legislative Councils sitting with well-sharpened pencils to record my advice on the next stage of the changes they had been elected to direct.

Of course, decolonization did not happen quite so easily as that. Respectable constitutionalists like the distinguished members of the Coussey Committee were not the only players on the field. After the Accra riots of 1948 Africans not included in any Colonial Office scenario began to grasp the intiative; and so, after the accession of Nkrumah's CPP to a position of power in the Gold Coast in 1951, an alternative historiography began to develop. African leaders (even including men who had formerly accepted the Imperial perspectives) now described their coming independence as the culmination of victorious struggles, proudly emphasizing that they too, like their Asian contemporaries and forerunners, could claim the valued status of "prison graduate". Increasingly too, they saw themselves within a lengthening perspective of pan-African political activity; this tradition received a classical exposition in *Pan Africanism or Communism?* published in 1956 by Nkrumah's Trinidadian associate George Padmore, veteran pan-African and former agent of the Third International.

Some struggles had been genuine enough, and many of the leaders of the succession states had wounds to show. Nkrumah, and many of his CPP colleagues, had known detention and prison; in Cameroun in 1945 and 1955, in Ivory Coast in 1949. Africans had been shot while resisting reactionary offensives by French *colons*; Senegalese ex-servicemen in 1944, Nigerian miners in 1949, became martyrs to the anti-colonial cause. But, as Lord Caradon retorted to Azikiwe in 1949,[7] these convulsions did not compare, in violence or duration, with those of contemporary Asian or North African nationalists; except in the early stages in Ghana and the final stages in Guinea, the transfer of power from European to African hands was smoother than the inheritors generally admitted. Many of the prosperous Ministers, officials and academics who endorsed the new historiography of liberation had – as such subsequent tragedies as the Nigerian Civil War made only too clear – accepted independence before directly confronting the old intractable problems left unresolved by the colonial rulers, or the new ones created by their withdrawal. Foreign observers – including Black Americans, greeted with patronizing enquiries about the progress of *their* independence struggles – soon began to perceive the limitations of "national bourgeoisies" who had not only inherited the privileges and perquisites of their former oppressors, but created new ones for themselves in the name of equality. To candid friends of West Africa, the new orthodoxy began to look inadequate, and some other interpretation of post-war developments seemed necessary.

So far, however, no alternative interpretation has displaced the assumption of the new West African establishment that the decisive victories have already been won. Not very many West Africans seem to read Frantz Fanon, the psychiatrist from Martinique who died in the service of the Algerian revolution, whose analysis fundamentally challenges such complacency. For Fanon, successful decolonization implies "a whole social structure being changed from the bottom up",[8] through the mobilization of the universal proletariat of "natives" – the *damnés de la terre*. His pessimism about the Africa of 1960 reflected experience not only of oppressed Algeria, but of "liberated" nations farther south; "the pitfalls of national consciousness" in new states lay mercilessly exposed in his finest chapter. Yet, within West Africa, only the PAIGC of Guiné-Bissau seems to have taken seriously Fanon's analysis, let alone his grim prescription of violence; only they can claim to have liberated their country in the fullest sense. (And even here, the final victory which Africans had prepared was won by the Portuguese revolution of 1974, so that the struggle ended with the new régime going through the hurried motions of decolonization.)

Southern Africa may yet be another story; but it remains ironical that Fanon's influence has been much greater among disillusioned bourgeois in Europe and the USA than among that proletariat of the Third World whose voice Jean-Paul Sartre proclaimed him to be. No *new* wind of change has blown through the former French and British colonies of West Africa since the one which obliged Harold Macmillan to change his clothes in 1960. Even the violence of the Nigerian Civil War had only limited "cleansing" effects; by 1974 unresolved issues of the First Republic re-emerged in bitter squabbling over the validity of a census which stood to determine the future distribution of wealth, power and perquisites, and Gowon's military government took the opportunity to abandon its pledge to restore civilian rule in 1976. It still remains to be seen whether a new constitution, drafted with scrupulous care, can provide a framework adequate to contain the explosive development of Nigeria's great human resources.

To understand the ambiguities and contradictions of contemporary West Africa we need to resolve ambiguities in our own interpretation of the conditions in which political independence arrived. So this discussion will now pass from historiography to history, to consider how far research, and the passage of time, are likely to bring any more convincing synthesis out of these simplified versions of "decolonization" and "liberation".

INTERNATIONAL PRESSURES AND THE IMPACT OF THE DEPRESSION

Synthesis, for some, implies a dialectical relationship; and the two forces of decolonization and liberation did exist, and interact significantly. Over-simple though the old historiographical assumptions may be, Britain and France *did* have intentions, sometimes even plans, to make the retention of formal empire unnecessary;

Africans *did* organize to challenge the measures prescribed for them, and to seize the initiative. What determined the relative strength of the two forces, the timing of events, the eventual conditions of political withdrawal, was not only social and political conditions within the different colonies (perhaps these determined the *sequence* of accession to independence) but the international context. West Africa, though rarely at the storm centre of the great confrontations of the twentieth century, has been as directly influenced by them as any quarter of the world.

Although the movement towards West African independence began to gather force in the 1930s, the origins can be traced much further back. Recent research has shown that Padmore was right to begin his account of pan-Africanism in the eighteenth century; indeed there was a great deal more early African thought and activity than even Padmore knew. The attempts of early West African intellectuals to retain some meaningful sense of African identity while consciously or unconsciously working to remake their countries after Western models certainly make a fascinating study, and one with a political dimension. Their petitioning and pamphleteering could modify policies of colonial governments in important particulars – especially if, as in the campaign of the Aborigines' Rights Protection Society in the Gold Coast against land legislation proposed in the 1890s, dangers of more direct resistance by rural Africans were latent in the background. Yet African independence, even if proclaimed as an ultimate goal, seemed to recede rather than approach during the last third of the nineteenth century. The Report of the British Parliamentary Committee of 1865, often quoted as a clear commitment to eventual decolonization, was never translated into practical measures or plans; and once policies of inland expansion were launched it was regarded as irrelevant by all except a few literal-minded Africans. Similarly, the hesitant steps of the Second and Third Republics to apply the famous 'policy of assimilation' to the government of Senegal were primarily designed to give political rights to resident Frenchmen, even though a few thousand mulattoes and Africans became incidental beneficiaries. After the imperialist offensives of the 1890s there was no early likelihood of either empire devolving power (as distinct from conceding limited influence) to the nationalist elite, and few Africans had serious hopes of compelling them to do so.

Some scholars see the First World War as marking a decisive turn on the road to colonial freedom; and in Asia its impact was clearly enormous. Here, forces for liberation had already been developing before 1914; the successful self-modernization of Japan, her victory over Russia in 1905, the Chinese Revolution of 1911, all stimulated nationalistic movements in India, Indonesia, Indo-China, Persia, Egypt and Algeria, and to varying degrees their spokesmen had established bases of popular support within their societies. International pressures generated by the Bolshevik revolution and by the liberal anti-imperialism of Woodrow Wilson intensified the pressure for reform in Asia; and some nationalist movements were able to claim political rewards for services rendered to the Allies by Asian servicemen, non-combatant auxiliaries, workers and peasants. Most notably, the British government in 1917 pledged itself to responsible government as the ultimate objective of its rule in India; but it must be remembered that there was no real consensus among British politicians upon such commitments to decolonization, and that their effect was counter-balanced by the actual expansion of colonial empires through the partition of Turkey, as well as of the German colonies.

In Black Africa, the pressures for liberation and decolonization alike were much more weakly felt. Africans had indeed become drawn into the war as soldiers and carriers. In particular, more than 160,000 soldiers were recruited from French West Africa, after strong resistance and severe repression; their services and lives were the price paid for the confirmation of citizen rights which the African Deputy Blaise Diagne was able to secure in 1916 for his constituents in the four communes of Senegal. On their return, ex-servicemen sometimes pressed more directly for social or political change. In south-eastern Dahomey in 1923 they joined dissident Muslims, transport workers, dynastic politicians, and radical journalists in strikes and demonstrations;[9] in Kenya they made up the nucleus of the Young Kikuyu Association formed by Harry Thuku in 1921. African societies were certainly not static; apart from such growth points as ports, administrative centres and mines, the cocoa-farming areas were already producing new groups of articulate rural entrepreneurs. But those centres of social change remained sufficiently weak, and sufficiently far removed from the sources of dangerous doctrines, to permit governments to isolate the mass of their subjects from advocates of revolution.

With no really sustained threat to the fabric of public order in view, there was no incentive to plan for decolonization, as distinct from reform. The establishment of the mandate system of the League, though not very effective as a continuing control upon colonial autocracy, did stimulate some administrators to rethink the moral justification of colonial rule – hence such treatises as Lugard's *Dual Mandate* (1922), and Albert Sarraut's *La Mise en Valeur des Colonies* (1923). What actual benefits followed depended largely on resources available; the prosperity of Gold Coast cocoa during the 1920s enabled Governor Guggisberg to initiate developments which earned him a substantial measure of African confidence. In West Africa, fewer expatriate interests were present than elsewhere, and colonial governments could reasonably claim to be acting as effective trustees for African interests – though even here their record was more vulnerable in questions affecting the localized labour requirements of mining companies and European planters, or the commercial interests of great oligopolies like the United Africa Company and the *Compagnie française de l'Afrique Occidentale*. In general, administrators remained confident that their subjects would continue to accept their authority, if humanely exercised, for an indefinite time to come.

Many retained this confidence into the 1930s, but with less reason. West Africa now experienced the full force of the international economic depression which, as Dr Hopkins has emphasized, reversed the generally expansionist tendencies which had hitherto determined the growth of the commercial sector of the colonial economies, and the fortunes of both Africans and Europeans who were involved in it.[10] Not only did the value and volume of West Africa's foreign trade decline sharply, but during the period 1930–44 the barter terms of trade deteriorated, so that even those who were able to sell the same quantity of palm-oil or cocoa could buy fewer imports than formerly with the proceeds. African producers and middlemen began to resort to radical action to defend their standard of living against the foreign oligopolies – not necessarily in the first place through the political organizations of the small national bourgeoisie, but through such direct action as large-scale cocoa hold-ups in the southern Gold Coast in 1937–8. At the same time colonial governments found their tax revenues greatly diminished, while the burden of interest charges remained fixed; fierce economy drives checked the progress of such modest programmes of development or welfare provision as they had attempted. The effect upon the complacency of those responsible for colonial policy was most clearly felt in the West Indies; in 1939 Lord Moyne's Commission painted so depressing a picture of the contradiction between "this new demand for better conditions [and] the unfavourable economic trend"[11] that its report was suppressed until the end of the war.

Internal stagnation coincided with serious external pressures. The threat of Communism, perceived since the Russian Revolution and the Comintern Manifesto of March 1919, was frequently exaggerated by imperial governments; in West Africa, unlike Asia, it was still practicable largely to insulate the people from such dangerous doctrines. Panicky officials often saw Red menaces among, for example, African admirers of the demagogic pan-African Marcus Garvey, whose reputation within Africa was widespread. Except in the Union, where a South African Communist Party was established under white leadership, the Third International had to struggle to establish contact with Africans through expatriates in Europe and America. Organizations under Comintern patronage introduced Black leaders like Padmore, Garan Kouyaté, Jomo Kenyatta, and I. T. A. Wallace-Johnson to radical critiques of imperialism and to Leninist methods of revolutionary organization. But after the shift of Comintern policy in 1933, even they became wary of revolutionaries whose tactical priorities clearly centred in Europe; their own emphasis was on establishing an independent and radically anti-colonial pan-African movement, especially after the USSR adopted an ambivalent position towards Italy's invasion of Ethiopia. Small though they were, these cosmopolitan contacts represented channels through which the constitutional protests of the 'national bourgeoisie' might become radicalized; contemporary developments in Asia illustrated the danger of writing off political movements of the educated elite as stage-armies of unrepresentative minorities.

Right-wing dictatorships presented different challenges to imperial complacency. Ever since the nineteenth century many West Africans had been conscious that the military power of Japan might one day be turned against European empires, and many welcomed the prospect; but Hitlerite racialism seemed less likely to win African support. (Nevertheless there was sufficient evidence of pro-German feeling in her former colonies to induce the French government in 1938 to relax its prohibition of political organization among the Camerounian elite in order to build up a loyalist connection called *Jeunesse Camerounaise Française*.) But the most direct danger to the West African empires was that the imperial governments themselves might be frightened into abandoning their colonies. When about 1938 some Ministers in Britain and France began to play with schemes of colonial appeasement,[12] those whose interests or ideals rebelled at this were impelled to think more seriously about how their continued rule might be rendered more acceptable and beneficial; and, in the longer term, about the conditions in which it might eventually be terminated. The statement by Malcolm MacDonald quoted earlier was made in reply to a Labour motion deploring any transfer of colonial territory without consent of the inhabitants.

Reforming impulses did not operate primarily through the channels of party politics. Although most leading European critics of colonial imperialism belonged to the Left, colonial affairs remained a minority interest there, and the interested minorities tended to specialize on countries whose demands seemed more urgent than those of West Africa – on India or North Africa, for example. Moreover, the thrust of anti-colonialism was divided: some critics concentrated on attacking the fact of alien rule, others on ensuring that power was more constructively exercised. (Many Western Social Democrats unconsciously imitated the Bolsheviks, who after promising the right of self-determination to the colonial slaves of Tsarism proceeded to reconstruct their societies in such a way that this right could be exercised only in ideologically acceptable directions.) However sincere the assertion of the right of Africans to govern themselves, goodwill alone provided no practical prescription for transferring control of the bureaucratic structures created by colonialism to peoples whose own institutions still worked on radically different principles. Hence all who accepted responsibility as "trustees", from the paternalist Right to the Communist Left, assumed that liberation would have to be preceded by a period of reform and improvement, during which the colonial authorities would identify, encourage and train African leaders willing and able to guide the post-colonial state in acceptable directions. Immediately, therefore, what needed to be done was to establish enlightened administration dedicated to long-term purposes of development and welfare.

So during the inter-war period Socialists and radicals found they could join in the discussion of practical programmes with political opponents, enlightened administrators, and a slowly-growing body of informed individuals – missionaries, a few academics less blinkered than their colleagues, some businessmen. The evolution of new policies provides a good example of changes formulated and directed by what has been called a "policy-making elite."[13] In France, the initiative seems to have developed within the colonial service itself; the *Ecole Coloniale* under Maurice Delafosse had become a centre of semi-academic debate about reformed principles of Native Administration while in the 1930s there was growing pressure within the service for more active programmes of social and economic development. Under the Popular Front government of 1936 these reforming tendencies were reinforced by political pressure for some modest enlargement of civic liberties and limited representation for *evolué* opinion; the Socialist Colonial Minister Marius Moutet relaxed some of the more oppressive measures of authoritarian control, proposed a new fund for economic development, and appointed an impressive (though in practice ineffective) committee of politicians, administrators and independent critics to study colonial problems. Though opposition in the colonies and parsimony in Parliament limited the effectiveness of this programme, the reforms now contemplated survived the fall not only of the Popular Front but of the Third Republic and re-emerged, strengthened, in the Brazzaville programme of 1944.

In the UK too there was increasing dialogue amongst those limited groups of people who were not content that African policy should stand still in the changing world. The 'Round Table' group of idealistic disciples of Milner, for example, initially looked for inspiration to the sphinx-like figure of Smuts; men like Lionel Curtis and Lord Lothian were anxious to apply the funds bequeathed by Rhodes to encourage research and discussion of African problems by British academics and practitioners. The Colonial Office for its part began to look for advice on the increasingly complex tasks of colonial government to missonaries, anthropologists and academics; thus its Advisory Committee on Native Education in the Imperial African Dependencies, which when established in 1924 was composed largely of former administrators, became progressively broadened. The few active political critics of empire of the older generation (J. A. Hobson, E. D. Morel, Josiah Wedgwood) had tended to maintain attitudes of critical independence towards the Colonial Office; but from the 1930s younger colonial specialists like Arthur Creech Jones increasingly began to discuss programmes of reform with other interested groups and individuals in departmental committees, and in such unofficial meeting places as Chatham House or the Royal Empire Society. From such discussions there emerged a consensus on the need for more active imperial policies to promote colonial development and welfare; the Bill establishing a fund for this purpose, prepared by Malcolm MacDonald under the Chamberlain government, was one of the first measures enacted by the Coalition during the crisis of May 1940.

EFFECTS OF THE SECOND WORLD WAR

Reformers of the 1930s placed the emphasis on countering the effects of the Depression and satisfying the material aspirations of Africans, rather than on accelerated decolonization. But soon after the outbreak of war MacDonald asked Lord Hailey – whose massive *African Survey*, published in 1938, had originated in the desire of the policy-making elite to ground African policy upon surer foundations of knowledge – to undertake a wide-ranging enquiry into matters relevant to possible political changes in post-war Africa. Much of Hailey's report concerned the status of the "Native Authorities" which were the principal agencies of local administration (it formed the basis of treatises which were later officially published); but the introductory chapter of his confidential report ranged much more widely.[14] Writing with authority derived from long Indian service, Hailey upset many preconceptions by declaring his outstanding impression of Africa to be "one of rapid change, and of greater changes impending"; "Can we", he asked, "be sure of the continuance of that degree of acquiescence in our rule which is a necessary condition of administrative progress?" He foresaw a continuing growth of pan-African racial sentiment, and of the political importance of the growing middle class, often belittled by the "Indirect Rulers". Though his specific recommendations were cautious, Hailey saw political advance as a necessary complement to the policies of development and welfare to which the government was already committed; and as wartime developments within West Africa gave added point to many of his prophecies, the Colonial Office increasingly turned its attention to preparing for political reform also.

This did not yet imply the early acceptance of African independence. Churchill, when pressed to apply the Atlantic Charter to the British Empire, refused to do so; the restoration of independence to conquered Europe, he told the Commons on 9 September 1941, was "quite a separate problem from the progressive evolution of self-governing institutions in the regions and peoples which owe allegiance to the British Crown". On this, he claimed, unambiguous declarations had been made, adapted to the special circumstances of the territories concerned. But official researches failed to produce any comprehensive set of such declarations, and the Colonial Office preferred to express its relationship with the colonies through the metaphor of "senior and junior partners in the same enterprise" – a phrase publicized by Hailey in the Lords on 20 May 1942, which was broad enough to embrace established development policies as well as the new inclination to seek political change. This concept of partnership seems to have been floated with the conscious aim of pre-empting American attempts to impose international controls on European colonies after the war by extending the older metaphor of trusteeship; Britain intended to retain sovereign control of her colonial policy, even while that policy was moving towards an accelerated decolonization.[15]

It may help us to understand this shift of policy if we think of colonial empire not, as our fathers may have done, as representing the normal relationship between Europeans and Africans, but as one particular historical form in which the inequality of power that has characterized that relationship in recent centuries has been expressed. Just as many historians now see the early nineteenth century as a period of "informal empire", when Britain enjoyed many of the perquisites of power in West Africa without the responsibilities of rule, so the period of "decolonization" may be seen as one of attempts to return to a somewhat similar position. Marx had seen the "double mission" of British rule in India as "the annihilation of old Asiatic society, and the laying of the material foundations of Western Society". In the 1940s, it was clearly premature to claim that any such mission had been accomplished in West Africa, but an implication of Hailey's assessment was that such a process was firmly launched. In face of the international pressures, it thus seemed feasible to accelerate the withering away of the formal apparatus of empire in the expectation that the former rulers would still retain sufficient economic, technological and cultural resources to exercise powerful influences upon future development.

Such a perspective need not imply any theory of conspiracy within the policy-making elites, with the cynical intention of creating neo-colonial relationships. Rather, these reformers saw themselves as modifying their paternalistic visions of the African future in order to accord with changing realities. But naturally, metropolitan interests still took a prominent place among these realities, especially in the post-war climate of continuing international economic disequilibrium and growing political tension. Economically, it seemed essential to retain some measure of control over the capacity of the colonies to produce scarce foods or raw materials – especially when, as in the case of cocoa from the Gold and Ivory Coasts, exports to the United States were helping to maintain the depleted gold and dollar reserves of the sterling and franc areas. In 1947 Sir Stafford Cripps could still exhort Colonial Governors to mobilize the resources of their territories for the sake of "the rehabilitation and strengthening of Western Europe".[16] Politically, an essential objective was to preclude any danger of African territories passing under Communist control; more immediately, French attempts to re-establish control in Indo-China were partially dependent upon African troops. Without such incentives to lay secure foundations for long-term relationships it may be doubted whether the British Parliament would in 1945 have been so ready to increase the limit of annual expenditure on Colonial Development and Welfare from £5 000 000 to £17 500 000, or whether the French Assembly would so readily have established the *Fonds d'investissement pour le développement économique et social* (FIDES) in 1946.

On such foundations of long-term and enlightened national interest, post-war governments elaborated increasingly comprehensive programmes for what Creech Jones, in a wide-ranging survey of 1946, called "the slow work of nation-building"[17] Up to the Accra riots of February 1948, constitutional reform was not the first priority of Britain's new African policies; constitutions introduced by Governor Richards in Nigeria in 1945, by Governor Burns in the Gold Coast in 1946, though providing for increased African representation and increased opportunities for these representatives to influence policy, by no means satisfied the nationalist elites. Nor were these appeased by early progress in the Africanization of the public service; in 1945 this new object of Imperial policy seemed quite compatible with large-scale recruitment of demobilized British officers for colonial careers, and the expanding responsibilities of colonial governments for providing development services prevented any spectacular increase in the proportion of Africans in senior official posts. In the long run the new African University Colleges were expected to provide cadres trained in the best British traditions; when recommending the establishment of these Colleges in 1945 the Elliot Commission had envisaged their role in educating the leaders of future African states, within a time-scale of between fifty and a hundred years.[18] Imaginatively far-sighted though they seemed at first, such predictions now became open to question.

In France, the political, administrative and economic priorities of the post-war years were somewhat different. Defeat had tended to polarize colonial administrators, no less than other sections of French society; but whereas those who followed Vichy adopted increasingly authoritarian, even racist, policies, the supporters of Free France did not envisage political independence. For de Gaulle the rallying of Equatorial Africa and Cameroun under the Black Guyanese Governor Félix Eboué in 1940 was an expression of confidence in continuing union between France and her colonies, which deserved to be rewarded by reforms in the spirit of 1936. Where the policies based on the Brazzaville programme of 1944 most closely resemble the programme of nation-building which Creech Jones had inherited from the wartime coalition is in the common emphasis on the social foundations with which the emergent African nations were to be endowed, with the help of development funds. Both looked beyond the political capitals to rural areas, and planned new local representative institutions at local levels (which it would prove difficult to graft on to old structures of native administration); programmes of community development, to be carried out under the watchful eyes of colonial administrators; the encouragement of voluntary associations of many types, including co-operatives and trade unions, which again were to be carefully guided in light of French or British experience. Given time, such innovations would lead to the emergence of good and stable societies, whose leaders would be influenced by values similar to those of the former ruling power; the eventual removal of imperial control would thus leave intact multiple bonds of common interest and ideology between European and Africans – cables along which messages would continue between former metropolis and former dependencies.

Political decolonization in West Africa was thus envisaged in 1945 as the culmination of wider programmes of reform; the "political kingdom" assumed priority only in so far as the colonial

Decolonization or Liberation?

empires came under international and internal pressures, economic, political and military. Self-government (in the British case), a more genuine assimilation (in the French), were accepted partly as a means of anticipating sustained opposition or resistance of the sort which both powers were experiencing elsewhere in their empires. Recognizing the pace of social change and the spread of political consciousness (which West Africa's role in wartime operations had accelerated in many ways), the governments aimed to keep the initiative in any conflicts which ensued, by encouraging the emergence of groups and classes of Africans who would be able and willing to lead their countries into the Commonwealth (or to fuller participation in the new French Union) with minimum prejudice to the interests and ideals of the Imperial Power.

Once this new emphasis in policy was established, progress towards decolonization was repeatedly expedited by far-sighted colonial officials who were sensitive to the changing mood of their African subjects. As Chief Secretary in Nigeria from 1947 to 1951, Lord Caradon (Sir Hugh Foot) was notably eager to earn the confidence and collaboration of the Nigerian leaders who had emerged under the "Richards Constitution"; he inspired the work of two predominantly Nigerian committees, one established in May 1948 to expedite Nigerianization of the public service, the other in March 1949 to accelerate the next phase of constitutional reform. Lord Caradon has emphasized that these were not responses to directions from Westminster, but spontaneous moves by men on the spot who sensed an urgent need to retain the initiative, once the Accra riots had warned them how rapidly they might come to be challenged by new movements from below. French officials too generally recognized the colonial reforms of 1945–6 as timely; and rapidly came to accept that developments within and outside Africa made it necessary to go beyond them.[19] Sensitive officials began to look more sympathetically towards leaders of the old elite who, like Azikiwe, Awolowo, Houphouët-Boigny or Danquah, had previously been distrusted as dangerous radicals.

Colonial rule had always depended upon the more or less voluntary collaboration of Africans in many capacities – as peasantry and proletariat, as chiefs, clerks, and other official intermediaries between alien rulers and subjects, even as licensed critics within the system. Now the quickening pressures for political change were making it necessary to extend the field of collaboration – or, to use the more acceptable term, of partnership –

to involve a new political and administrative class who would work for the gradual creation of self-governing African polities, with reconstructed societies and institutions.

THE SUDDEN DEATH OF WEST AFRICAN COLONIALISM.

These imperial initiatives, increasingly directed towards a formal transfer of political power, provide a logical point of departure for a historical explanation of West African independence. At present, such an explanation can be offered only in general and tentative terms. At every point there is a need for further research; new evidence and changing perspectives brought about by the passage of time are likely to change these perspectives very drastically. As suggested earlier, Africans willing to collaborate, to act as partners in the new policies, soon came forward; but within a few years many (not all) of them were overtaken, over-shadowed, or forced to shift their own ground by the emergence of new leaders, drawing support from much broader sections of West African society – Nkrumah from unemployed school-leavers or ex-servicemen, frustrated cocoa – farmers and the traditional rural opposition of the 'young men', Sékou Touré from trade unionists, and those who suffered under the chiefly bureaucracy imported by the French. Naturally and obviously enough, these sectors of rapid social change provided the most effective thrusts for political liberation from below. Growing militancy in the two southern regions of Nigeria, the increasingly strong challenge to French trusteeship of the *Union des Peuples du Cameroun*, and the gradual formation of a mass party organization in Guinea, all reinforced the warning that the dangers of rapid decolonization might be less than those of excessive caution.

For Britain, a critical moment arrived after Nkrumah's return to the Gold Coast in December 1947. Initially his tone and language, coupled with some known political associations, made British officials fear a Communist conspiracy; the Accra riots of 28 February 1948, closely following the Communist seizure of power in Czechoslovakia and coinciding with increasing fears of Communist insurrection in Malaya (the other main dollar-earning colony), provoked panicky initial reactions which identified the nationalists as puppets in the Cold War. But a new and stronger Governor, Sir Charles Arden-Clarke, soon realized that the new militants could still be persuaded to collaborate in the work of decolonizing, and that timely concessions would actually reduce the danger of Soviet involvement; even while Nkrumah was imprisoned in 1950 it became accepted that eventually it would be necessary to work with his Convention Peoples' Party. For the French, a turning-point came in the Ivory Coast in 1949; the brief but bloody confrontation between a reactionary administration and the followers of Houphouët-Boigny (then an open fellow-traveller of the French Communist Party) made both parties change course, recognizing that their essential interests might after all be reconciled through negotiated collaboration.

Hence, only in Cameroun did West African liberation movements need to embark on prolonged armed struggles. Although elsewhere in their empires – in Indo-China and Algeria, in Malaya, Kenya and Aden – French and British governments judged it necessary to fight popular movements in defence of economic or strategic interests, in West Africa they judged it possible and prudent to manoeuvre. In order to keep the initiative, and the prospect of influence within the succession states, they were prepared to abandon old collaborators (like the members of the Coussey Committee) in favour of new leaders, despite the apparent radicalism of their programmes (and to grant unexpected concessions to the old).

Although this political acceleration was inaugurated under the Attlee government, it did not become politically controversial; its principal strategist appears to have been Andrew Cohen of the Colonial Office, who grasped the necessity of adjusting the new approaches evolved by the policy-making elite to changing conditions. A few right-wing Conservatives complained but there was no real opposition from the party leadership; and when Oliver Lyttelton took over the Colonial Office in 1951, little change was apparent in the instructions to West African Governors. In France too, where the domestic political situation of the Fourth Republic was much less stable, politicians who cared about colonial problems had more pressing crises to worry about. On West African issues pressures from the Communist allies of African deputies and from the spokesmen of settler and business interests tended to cancel each other out; successive governments thus embarked on a sequence of measures which, increasingly though almost imperceptibly, diverged from the insistence of the Brazzaville programme that the establishment of "self-governments" was excluded.

In the euphoric atmosphere which these apparently successful exercises in decolonization produced during the 1950s, it was easy to forget that this reversal of priorities meant abandoning or overlooking many of the assumptions about the social foundations of good government on which colonial officials had framed their development programmes. To take one example: in 1948 the Sierra Leone government appointed a Provincial Commissioner, an Agricultural Officer and a forester to prepare recommendations concerning soil conservation and land use. Many of their comprehensive and detailed proposals – concerning the introduction of more scientifically-based procedures into what is called "the conservative and independent outlook of the farmer"[20] and the extension and more efficient management of forest reserves – assumed a period of administrative stability for their application; but during the 1950s these unromantic essentials were over-shadowed by an extraordinary diamond rush, and by the Colonial Office policy of synchronizing the transfer of political power with events in Ghana and Nigeria. Former colonial servants can multiply examples, and many express regret that constitutional changes could not be deferred until improved communications had reduced social disparties between villages of the interior and cities of the plain, until swollen shoot had been eliminated from cocoa farms, until the new elite of African graduates had permeated the public service and the political nation. During the 1950s the British and French governments in turn made concessions to African pressures which in the previous decade would have seemed intolerably rash. But under the economic and political constraints of the Cold War period the risks seemed necessary – and justifiable by the hope of finding African successors who would "talk the same language" and recognize the same goals.

The tactical flexibility was possible because, in West Africa, French and British interests were secondary. Elsewhere in Africa, political decolonization excited profound conflicts of interest within the metropolitan society, and sometimes these could not be resolved until the force of African liberation movements had been brought to bear in Europe. The most spectacular example of this is of course provided by the Algerian war of 1954–62. Initially, all major French parties assumed that the union of France and Algeria had to be maintained in one form or another; the achievement of the FLN was not merely to shake France's military control and to lay the foundations of revolution in Algeria, but to transform the face of

France itself. Among their indirect achievements they could claim to have overthrown the Fourth Republic, to have threatened the Fifth with civil war and to have radicalized the thinking of the French Left on a whole range of questions concerning relations with the Third World. But the connection between events in Algeria and in AOF should not be forgotten. On the one hand, France's readiness to accept the political reforms which led from the *loi-cadre* of 1956 to the independences of 1960 was clearly influenced by the need to avoid further military commitments on Algeria's southern borders; but in turn the apparent initial success of this exercise in decolonization made the prospect of Algerian independence less unthinkable. "With luck, Houphouët-Boigny; at worst, Sékou Touré," de Gaulle is said to have stoically commented as he contemplated France's political withdrawal from Algeria.

In a similar way, West African experience facilitated changes in British policy in Eastern and central Africa. Until the late 1950s the presence here of settler minorities (strongly connected by interest, blood and sentiment with British Conservatives) seemed to exclude political decolonization, unless on the basis of some unequal "partnership" which would ensure their continuing control. (Such a system was the objective of the ill-fated Central African Federation of 1953, a move which originally had support in both major British political parties.) The Mau Mau rising in Kenya, though fed by genuine anti-colonial grievances, could not be recognized as a legitimate struggle for political freedom, and Britain's commitment to its suppression seemed to imply continued political control. But the costs of this campaign made it all the more expedient to transfer power to African hands not only in West Africa but in Uganda, and in the Trust territory of Tanganyika; and the apparent success of decolonization in Ghana made policy-makers in Britain increasingly wary of the dangers of attempting to pursue such contradictory policies in Africa. In 1959 widespread disturbances in Nyasaland compelled the Macmillan government to undertake far-reaching changes of policy which – at the price of considerable pain within the Conservative Party – included the accelerated transfer of power to African majorities in Kenya as well as Uganda, Tanganyika and Zanzibar, the demolition of the Central African Federation, and the abandonment of the attempt to incorporate African nations within the same Commonwealth as the increasingly racist Republic of South Africa.

2 Wartime Origins of Political Transfer

After 1865, the year of an often-quoted and often-misunderstood Parliamentary Committee, the transfer of power in British West Africa was a subject to which less thought was given in Great Britain than among Africans. For supporters of empire, the question was removed from the agenda when vast new imperial commitments were undertaken during the partition. Among the critics, anti-imperialists who aimed at the destruction of colonial empire were always fewer and less effective than those who aimed to transform colonial dominance into juster (and so potentially more durable) forms of relationship. Under economic and political pressures during the inter-war years, the ideas and programmes of colonial reformers began increasingly to penetrate the "policy-making elite". The Colonial Development and Welfare Act of 1940 crowned the first phase of a major re-appraisal. But despite political rhetoric concerning gradual progress towards self-government, ambiguity persisted about the political goals towards which the new "planned colonial policy" would lead West Africa; economic and social development could equally well culminate with their closer incorporation into the Empire-Commonwealth system as in a transfer of political power. At the outbreak of the Second World War, constitutional changes in central government remained very low on the working agenda of West African administrations.

The opening of official British archives allows us to study that agenda, and the gradual transformation of its priorities, with greater precision than before. Snap judgements on this subject may be dangerous; the Colonial Office, like all the machinery of British government, was growing increasingly complex in its internal organisation, and in its capacity to intervene in the colonies,[1] and essays like this which are based on evidence relating to a portion of the field are liable to find their perspective distorted. The first sections of this chapter nevertheless attempt to show how, under the intensive and complex pressures generated by the war, new constitutional policies were evolved. Although these reflected old aspirations of African leaders, the initiative in shaping them lay with the Colonial Office and the colonial governments; the schemes which they jointly devised were intended to mature over many years, in ways which would safeguard Britain's political principles as well as her interests. The war intensified the social pressures behind the African "nationalists", and the changing international situation gave them greater leverage; when the archives are more fully open they will show how British policies had to adjust to accelerations of time-table which radically altered their effects. But only rarely did Africans come near to capturing the initiative or controlling the process of change. Decolonizers and liberators both had to compromise, with results often evident in modern West Africa.

NATIVE ADMINISTRATION AND POLITICAL DEVELOPMENT

The new thinking generated by the Depression of the 1930s had largely been focused on "development policy" and the extension of social welfare, rather than on political change as a policy in itself. As far as West Africa is concerned, political thought centred on methods of applying Lugardian principles of indirect rule to native administration, their general suitability being taken for granted. In theory, indirect rule provided a framework within which the conflicting claims of "progress and security" could be reconciled in various ways; in practice, "security" usually won. At their best, Native Authorities were like vintage cars, elaborate and dignified structures with little capacity for acceleration, and strong tendencies to steer to the right. The great extensions now envisaged in the responsibilities of colonial government made it urgent to improve the capacity of such bodies to discharge them, and in the longer term raised the question of their role in an ultimate political future tacitly assumed to involve "self-government based on representative institutions".[2]

In practice the nature of "native administration", and hence the problems of replacing it, varied enormously (this is perhaps why no two scholars working on different parts of the African empire ever agree on the meaning of "indirect rule"). In Sierra Leone it was matter of patiently working to generate some modern administrative capacity in 216 impoverished chiefdoms with an average population of under 10 000; in 1935, £1500 was provided for "the experimental introduction of the system known as Native Administration, on Southern Nigerian lines, into selected chiefdoms".[3] In the Gold Coast Colony the need was felt to assert stronger central control over chiefs who, with their councillors, claimed to exercise "inherent rights" of government, and enjoyed effective control over the often very substantial revenues produced by the concession of stool-lands for cocoa-farming and gold-mining, and by consequent litigation.[4]

But if the first priority of colonial governments in the 1930s was to improve their capacity to rule, by creating reliable local agencies for the collection and expenditure of taxation within the new context of development policy, they also became more concerned to ensure that native authorities enjoyed consent from below. In Northern Nigeria this might not seem terribly urgent; but elsewhere many administrative officers saw an increasing need to supplement (or correct) the wisdom of the elders by that of traders, school-teachers, clerks, mammy-waggon proprietors – in other words by representatives of that nascent African middle class, which grew with every advance in the colonial economy, and experienced frustration with every check in the process. Radical reform of local institutions seemed essential if these were to carry the administrative strain of new developed policies.

Forward-looking officials also saw that this might provide a means of gradually enlarging the system of "collaboration" on which the British West African empire rested. Not only the chiefs but also the leaders of the "national bourgeoisie" had hitherto retained and expressed a fervent "Empire loyalism", even in their political protests. This is remarkable, for the British Empire allowed educated Africans only limited and grudging access to a narrow range of professional and business opportunities, to the junior levels of public office, and to a narrowly circumscribed "sphere of civil usefulness" in selected towns. Nevertheless, the rhetoric of Commonwealth and Empire had encouraged such men to hope that they might one day inherit control of the colonial state. Hitherto this day had seemed too distant to be relevant to the daily concerns of busy colonial administrators who rarely took the rhetoric seriously anyhow. But if the collaboration of middle-class Africans was now required by new development policies, they might reasonably expect some clearer statement of their political prospects. The outbreak of war, which placed new demands on Africans for maintenance of ports and airfields, increased production of raw materials and service in the armed forces, made this still more urgent. Early perception of this lay behind the extended tour of British African colonies which Lord Hailey was asked to undertake in December 1939. His ostensible mission was to follow up his magisterial *African Survey* by more detailed study of Native Administration in the several colonies: but, as West African Governors were told, he was to do this in a wider political context:

> It may be that one of the results of the war will be to stimulate the political consciousness of Africans and to give emphasis to the demand for a quickened pace of development towards more representative and liberal institutions of government. In any case it seems very desirable from the standpoint of high policy that H.M.G. should attempt now to clarify in their own minds the important problem of the future development of unofficial African representation in Legislative Councils in relation to the evolution of indirect rule and the future development of native administration. Important decisions may have to be taken to prevent Native Administration on the one hand and Legislative Councils on the other from developing upon diverging lines.[5]

This did not imply any drastic shift of priorities from economic towards constitutional reform. Indeed the immediate effect of the war was to sharpen the British government's commitment to initiate and carry through long-term programmes of colonial development and reconstruction. In April 1941 Hailey, while still drafting his Report, was asked to chair a Colonial Office committee consisting of four Assistant Under-Secretaries with the wide remit of "post-war reconstruction in the colonies". The agenda[6] of over fifty headings which it produced had the effect of stimulating enquiry and formulation of views throughout the Office. Priority was given to economic problems likely to arise in the direct aftermath of war, and to improving the capacity of colonial governments to handle the technical problems of longer-term development. Constitutional and political matters were less prominent; and the general conclusions which Hailey drew from his mission did not provide unambiguous guidance.

In many ways, *Native Administration and Political Development in British Tropical Africa* is a far-sighted document. Hailey foresaw a continuing growth of "African racial consciousness' and of the influence of the African middle class: his Indian experience added extra weight to his perception of "rapid change, and of greater changes impending", and to his rhetorical question, "Can we be sure of the continuance of that degree of acquiescence in our rule which is a necessary condition of administrative progress?" But Hailey doubted whether acquiescence could be secured by what he disparagingly called "constitution-mongering"; his approach was rather to identify potential political and administrative elites who could gradually be trained to assume the enlarged responsibilities of the colonial state. As required by his brief, he concentrated upon the diverse problems of "native administration". While decisively rejecting the idea that, even in Northern Nigeria, Native Authorities were embryonic states with "inherent rights", which might become the direct heirs of colonial sovereignty, Hailey did regard them as the key, not only to efficient local government, but to constitutional advance.[7] When eventually it became necessary to reconstitute the central legislature, Regional Councils, based upon reformed authorities, would become channels for indirect election which could be trusted to return hard-headed men of the people.[8] Even the conservative Lord Moyne found this emphasis on "local tribal institutions" as the major channel of political advance and education over-cautious and "hardly democratic".[9]

The political philosophy implicit in Hailey's approach was still dominant in the Colonial Office and colonial service a year later, when his reports were printed for wide circulation among officials, and suitable persons outside.[10] But now the case for some clearer declaration of political intent had become much strengthened by disputes over the interpretation of the Atlantic Charter, by America's entry into the war, and by the traumatic shock of the fall of Singapore. Despite Churchill's well-known addiction to imperial ideas, it was essential to convince allies and potential allies that victory would bring positive benefits to Britain's colonial subjects; it was equally urgent to convince West Africans of this, as the demands of the war effort upon them were intensified. Statements of long-term policy would hardly do: nor even municipal reform, which few Africans accepted as a sufficient "sphere of civic usefulness". The need to supplement indirect rule by more imaginative gestures was understood by Sir Alan Burns, who, having served on Hailey's reconstruction committee during secondment to the Colonial Office, went to the Gold Coast as Governor in October 1941.

GOVERNOR BURNS, THE COLONIAL OFFICE AND THE GOLD COAST CONSTITUTION

Born in 1887 in St Kitts, in a third generation of colonial civil servants, Burns had divided a distinguished career between the Caribbean (he governed British Honduras 1934–40) and Nigeria (of which country in 1929 he published a *History* that is still frequently cited). Though paternalistic and even authoritarian in many of his attitudes (as might befit Lugard's former ADC),[11] Burns had acquired a reputation among his Colonial Office colleagues for an "ardent temperament" which was liable to express itself particularly strongly on matters of colour prejudice (on which subject he published a book in 1948).[12] A devout Catholic, he prided himself on his ability to co-operate with Africans according to their character and abilities – he later collaborated with an eminent Ghanaian in writing a pamphlet designed to reduce racial misunderstanding;[13] but by the same token he could react strongly against African politicians who failed to measure up to his own strict ethical standards. Though capable of expressing remarkably libertarian views for a Governor,[14] he found it difficult to maintain them if faced with a challenge to colonial authority, or colonial values. Nevertheless his abundant energy and good will, and his recognition that the times called for active imperial initiatives, would prove valuable assets during difficult years. Before leaving London he discussed with Moyne a range of desirable reforms: increased Africanization of senior posts (including some in District administration), ending of residential segregation, municipal reform, extended African representation in the Legislative Council, the appointment of African members to the Executive Council. Although warned that the latter points would require further consideration after discussion by the Governors' Conference, Burns was encouraged to "experiment" with proposals on these lines, and the important point was conceded that reforms for which the Gold Coast seemed ready should not be delayed solely on grounds that the time was unripe elsewhere in West Africa.[15]

On arriving in Africa Burns soon had to deal with serious strikes over the cost of living, in Nigeria as well as the Gold Coast, and this confirmed his resolve to press ahead with reforms.[16] His Africanization proposals were hailed by the Colonial Office as "sensible and moderate" (hence they proved less than adequate for the post-war expansion of the colonial state);[17] on residential segregation he fought a drawn battle against the contention of medical authorities in London and Africa that "the preservation of the health of the Europeans . . . is of such paramount importance that the political effect of racial segregation must be accepted as inevitable".[18] His first political initiative was to press a reluctant Colonial Office to agree to the appointment of African members of the Executive Council. Burns argued:

> I believe that the rising tide of anti-British resentment, and the disturbances which in recent years have been symptoms of this resentment, are due to the policy of deferring constitutional concessions until it is too late for them to be appreciated by the people. The Negro peoples, both in the West Indies and in West Africa, are learning that the colonial administrations take no notice of popular feeling until this feeling is manifested in disturbances.

Perceiving "a growing feeling of antipathy to Europeans and an under-current of discontent which affords a fertile field for the subversive activities of enemy agents", Burns, backed by Bourdillon from Nigeria, persisted against objections raised by Hailey and other Colonial Office pundits. In September Lord Cranborne, as Secretary of State, was persuaded to authorize such appointments, in Nigeria as well as the Gold Coast.[19] But these were gestures made by grace and favour; the crucial point for African opinion would be the recommendations for constitutional reform.

In his interview with Moyne, Burns had specifically suggested unofficial majorities only in municipalities, proposing an unspecified increase in African representation on the Legislative Council. By December 1942 however his mind was clearly moving towards accepting an unofficial majority there also,[20] no doubt hoping thus to turn aside African opposition to the introduction of income-tax, which the Colonial Office had just decided to impose against his advice.[21] This did not, however, indicate any intention to move towards an early transfer of power; even in 1949 Burns did not believe the Gold Coast was "yet fit for self-government".[22]

Unofficial majorities were to be linked with a re-affirmation and definition of the Governor's reserve powers; Caribbean experience led Burns to believe that such a system could work well, with little need to put these powers into practice. But the critical point was the link which Burns perceived between the future composition of the legislature and the distribution of power in the localities.

Hailey's reports had emphasized the need to apply the orthodox doctrines of indirect rule by establishing stronger control by the central government over the traditional states of the Colony; as in 1936 he rejected the alternative of subordinating the chiefs to elected local Councils as "an inevitable *pis aller* where . . . the chiefdoms had been smashed beyond hope of recovery". Burns accepted this objective, which he eventually implemented through the Native Authorities Ordinance of 1944. To overcome the resistance of the chiefs he worked to persuade their most influential leader, Sir Ofori Atta I of Akim Abuakwa, that they would be amply recompensed for their loss of autonomy by central government grants to the reformed authorities, and by increased representation at the centre under the new constitution.[23]

His experience during these difficult negotiations increased Burns's respect for the traditional rulers, and diminished his sympathy for the emergent bourgeoisie. He became openly contemptuous of many of the "intelligentsia" and "demagogues" with whom he had to deal, especially Ofori Atta's learned kinsman J. B. Danquah; in planning municipal reforms, which were to provide "training for the further political advance of the Gold Coast", he was anxious to minimize their influence. Whereas his proposal of July 1942 for a municipality in Kumasi envisaged half the members directly elected on an occupier franchise, by December he was temporarily flirting with a suggestion that the existing franchise in Accra should be abolished in favour of indirect elections through the traditional authorities.[24] Though he resisted that dangerous temptation, Burns had no intention of promoting a legislature dominated by such men.

A crucial point in plans for constitutional change was that the existing Legislative Council represented only the Colony; Asante and the Northern Territories (as well as the Togoland mandate) lay outside its competence. Hailey had recommended "as our ultimate objective the establishment of a Central Legislature, with three territorial councils"; and in February 1943 Burns took a step in this direction by proposals to establish in Advisory Council for Asante.[25]

But at this stage the Asantehene and his fellow-chiefs did not wish to be brought under the Central Legislature, nor to seek representation there; constitutional reform thus remained a matter of balancing different interests within the Colony, and Burns believed he had found the key in his bargain with Ofori Atta and the chiefs. But since the Colonial Office remained unconverted to unofficial majorities,[26] Burns made no formal proposal pending the planned visit to West Africa of Oliver Stanley, the new Secretary of State.

After Burns left London, Colonial Office thinking had continued to concentrate on long-term plans for economic, social and educational development rather than on constitutional reform. Some impetus was given in this direction by the appointment in May 1942 of Lord Swinton as Resident Minister in West Africa. This arose from the desire of the armed services for more direct means of influencing policy (they would have preferred a military Governor-General); but besides co-ordinating operational priorities and external relations Swinton presided over Governors' Conferences, reconstituted as the Civil Members Committee, and began to build up a policy-making capacity of his own. This was much strengthened after February 1943 when the West African Department, warmly encouraged by Stanley, decided to prepare what became known as a "planned policy for West Africa". O. G. R. Williams, of the West African Department, and Arthur Dawe, the Assistant Under-Secretary, argued that, as the danger of military operations receded, the Government should be prepared to confront an incipient agitation with a definite plan of action: "Our success in raising the standard of life, in the widest sense of the term, of the African is likely to be largely dependent upon the extent to which we can associate him as an active collaborator in the task of his own betterment."[27]

One aspect of this policy, to which Dawe attached greater priority than Williams, was the creation of a development staff at "Resmin" on the lines of the office of Comptroller set up in the West Indies after the Moyne report of 1939. Distinguished specialist advisers were appointed to serve all four colonies – Noel Hall on development, Maxwell Fry on town planning. In Swinton they had a shrewd and active political head who had been Secretary of State in 1931–5. On 24 February 1943 Swinton presented to the Civil Members Committee a comprehensive paper on economic policy, envisaging colonial governments pursuing very actively interventionist policies for an indefinite period after the war.[28] Swinton was

Wartime Origins of Political Transfer 33

strongly sceptical about the "Westminster model": his prescription was:

> Pressing on with the things that matter to the common man, agricultural and industrial development, co-operative farming and marketing, health, education; staffing the services concerned with Africans as quickly as they can be trained; assigning to African local administrators more and more responsibility for these services. The more Africans are playing their part in the things that really matter, the less they will bother about constitutional forms . . . .[29]

But the Colonial Office already knew that the increased social pressures of wartime would raise constitutional claims which "will then demand attention as being themselves factors in the immediate wartime situation";[30] Williams's memorandum emphasized expanded educational systems, Africanization of the public service, and gradual political change. Already during 1942 they had activated plans for a Commission on Higher Education in West Africa, which had been under leisurely discussion since the Governors' Conference in August 1939 had identified a West African University as "an ideal at which they should aim"; while still assuming that the Commission could not conduct its main enquiries in wartime, they decided to appoint a nucleus to begin work, under a Chairman who would recognize that (as Stanley put it when approaching Lord Harlech) "the most important aspects of the question are political".[31] During 1943 the full Commission (including three West African members) was in fact appointed, with Walter Elliot as chairman, and its active enquiries began later that year. The development of a high-class university was thus recognized, not only as a concession highly valued by the West African elite, but as a means of preparing technical, administrative and political cadres for future African states. But it was still assumed that decades must pass before these necessary preparations were complete. The time-scale within which a transfer of power seemed feasible was shortening, but would still allow plenty of opportunities for what Williams called the "progressive education of the African in the handling of public affairs".[32]

During the summer of 1943, while Stanley prepared for the first tour of the West African colonies ever undertaken by a Secretary of State, the Colonial Office attempted to clarify its views on this delicate question. On 20 July Stanley presided over a discussion of a paper by Williams. This voiced the still-prevalent caution about the "enormous gulf between groups of politically-minded Africans . . . and the vast bulk of African cultivators living under tribal conditions"; but, while foreseeing "deplorable results" if political concessions to the former group outran the "material or social development of the latter", Williams accepted Hailey's argument that the West African elite *did* need assurances that the progress would not be retarded to keep step with East Africa. His "tentative plan for constitutional development" was based on Hailey's proposals to reform local and regional government on foundations of indirect rule, but suggested five stages which might lead to political change at the centre. While the emphasis of the first stage would be largely on local government – the "gradual modernization" of Native Authorities being accompanied by increased African representation on Municipal Councils, and by the formation of advisory Regional Councils based on the N.A.s. – there would also be increased representation of African interests, by elected and nominated members, on Legislative Councils. Unexpectedly, Hailey himself proposed a further measure of "education in responsibility", intended to prevent educated Africans adopting the role of "chartered opposition": Africans should be appointed as heads of departments with seats in the Executive Council, though without full ministerial powers. Williams's second and third stages would consist largely of extending the functions of Regional Councils, together with measures to make both municipalities and Legislative Councils more directly representative. The fourth stage might see African unofficial majorities in Legislative Councils: but the Colonial Office was still unhappy about unofficial majorities without responsibility government, and also feared that Europeans in Eastern Africa might demand similar status. Williams therefore thought it might be desirable to move directly to Stage Five, somewhat tentatively entitled "towards self-government".[33]

Beyond the first stage, this was not really a "plan" at all, even a tentative one, but a well-guarded declaration of intent. Williams's paper was wholly imprecise about Stage Five, suggesting only that it would have to be preceded by a lot of consultation with African interests, and it was still accepted that despite the certainty of growing African pressure, "A good many years (perhaps a good many generations though it would be impolitic to say so openly) must elapse before the possibilities of stages 1, 2 and 3 have been at all fully exploited."[34] The immediate object was not to hasten constitutional proposals but to permit Stanley to give the African deputations he was about to receive general political reassurances (if hardly the unequivocal commitment which Hailey, on the basis of his Indian experience, was now suggesting). But before Stanley reached the Gold Coast, Williams's programme was called in question by an African initiative.

Among the papers prepared for presentation to Stanley was an impressive Petition signed by African members of the Asante Confederacy Council as well as of the Legislative Council and the Joint Provincial Council of Gold Coast Colony. Without questioning the ultimate authority of the Governor this called for an elected majority on the Legislative Council, with formal provision for members of that majority to be appointed to the Executive Council, and to a new "Ministry of Home Affairs".[35] Such a petition might have been politely pigeon-holed, but for what Burns called an "astonishing change" in the attitude of the Asantehene and his Councillors, who now requested early representation for their country on the Legislative Council. To resist this request might jeoparadize the basis of collaborative rule in Asante; but if it was accepted the existing official majority of one could be maintained only by reducing the representation of other elements or by adding more officials – both courses certain to arouse African hostility. Burns therefore urged Stanley to agree to the unofficial majority – "the one demand that will really satisfy the politically-minded people in this country" – so that he could resist more dangerous claims for a footing in the executive.[36] Burns's political strategy had been shaken by the death on 20 August of Ofori Atta, whose collaboration was the key to reform of the Native Authorities, and by the rising influence of the detested J. B. Danquah; this unforced gesture of political intent seemed the best way to regain the initiative.

This suggestion of course ran counter to the strategy of Williams's five stages, and the first reaction of the Office was that it would be a "lesser evil" to match Asante representation by appointing additional official members.[37] But Stanley's discussion with Burns in Accra, and his discovery that Bourdillon in Nigeria and Blood in The Gambia also favoured unofficial majorities subject to reserve powers, removed his opposition. The argument that African unofficial majorities in the West might set precedents for Europeans on the other side of the continent was over-ridden, and Burns was authorized to elaborate constitutional proposals which he had already drafted as an alternative to those in the Danquah petition.[38] While African appointments to the Executive Council were still to be at the Governor's discretion, the Legislative Council would now have a substantial African majority: this would consist primarily of members indirectly elected through advisory councils for Asante and the Colony, reconstituted on the basis of the new Native Authority legislation which was simultaneously being prepared. (The Northern Territories would temporarily be represented only by their Chief Commissioner.) In May 1944 Burns visited London and secured Stanley's agreement to negotiations on this basis with African representatives, "but on the distinct understanding that apart from the four municipal members [it had been agreed to accept direct elections in Kumasi] . . . the form of election would be substantially that at present in force in the case of the six Provincial members."[39] Unofficial majorities, in other words, were acceptable only on safe foundations of indirect rule.

The basis of a new pattern of collaboration now seemed laid. At two meetings in July and August with African members of existing Councils Burns made a number of detailed concessions, and in return secured their cordial consent, not only to the new constitution which was to bear his name, but to the Native Authorities legislation. Stanley himself had now grasped the symbolic importance of the unofficial majority, and was anxious not to jeopardize the good atmosphere its acceptance had created by delay in preparing new constitutional instruments.[40] The change was not expected to involve any significant shift of power; a contemporary regarded Burns's handling of public opinion as "not so much consultation as education", and did not expect the new Council to "assert its independence in obstructive or unco-operative ways".[41] But Burns had fundamentally changed the stages of Colonial Office planning, and it was necessary to consider implications for the other West African colonies.

Nigeria was of course the critical case. It was far the largest and potentially most important of the British dependencies, and political activists in the South were no less articulate and active (if no more effectively united) than their Gold Coast contemporaries. But the very size and complexity of the country made it unsuited for political experiment, especially since the way indirect rule had developed in the North had created powerful interests opposed to the sort of changes under discussion in the South. Conservative political doctrines were powerfully held by British officials in the North; Chief Commissioner Sir Theodore Adams, an ex-Malayan official, aimed to promote the autonomous development of the Emirates as "Protected States", and believed "the policy of a central African Government incompatible with the Emirate system".[42] Such views were rejected by Sir Bernard Bourdillon, Governor 1935-43, though less categorically than by Hailey. Bourdillon, believing the basis of Nigerian opposition to colonial rule to be "99 per cent economic", had been an early advocate of a vigorous development policy, for which Nigerian unity provided the appropriate administrative framework. Instead of trying to exclude southerners from the North, the Emirs should be encouraged to demand their own "finger in the Nigerian pie", taking their place along with the "progressives" in the central legislature.[43] But if immediate steps were to be taken to constitute political unity it could only be on the basis of the diverse regional structures which indirect rule had fortified. That this would ensure the dominant influence of conservative British advice during the gradual process of political advance was a welcome corollary.

Since 1939 Bourdillon had favoured the creation of advisory councils with legislative and financial powers within the three existing regions, and had regarded these as the basis for gradual constitutional change at Lagos. As Hailey pointed out there was nothing "natural" about these regions; developing them as political authorities might create conflicts and Bourdillon himself thought the structure should be thoroughly re-examined.[44] But any serious administrative reconstruction would have tended to delay constitutional change, and events in the Gold Coast during 1943 made this undesirable. At a meeting in the Colonial Office in November 1943 Bourdillon's designated successor, Sir Arthur Richards, accepted his general approach (although, having been briefed by Adams, he emphasized the need for cautious handling of the Emirs, who retained the key to British authority in the North). But Stanley, fresh from his African tour, pointed out that the confidence of the "Lagos politicians" was also relevant; he pressed Richards towards granting an unofficial majority in the new Legislative Council in order to keep in step with developments in the Gold Coast.[45] The basic foundations of the famous "Richards Constitution", including its transformation of administrative regions into embryonic states, were thus laid before the new Governor arrived in Nigeria.

The implications for constitutional change in the smaller West African colonies seemed less urgent, and less clear. "It would be obviously absurd to think of all the existing Colonial units as being equally fit for self-government," Williams had written in his paper of 1943; no doubt the slender territorial, economic and demographic resources of The Gambia were uppermost in his mind, but Sierra Leone seemed hardly better able to meet vague Colonial Office criteria of "viability", and the social foundations on which political progress would have to rest were seriously defective. Reform of the chiefdoms, which was to form the grass roots of political progress, was proceeding slowly and unimpressively; and the Creoles, no longer regarded as suitable collaborators and heirs to Empire, were commonly despised and rejected. Stanley, who had been depressed by his visit to Freetown, accepted Governor Hubert Stevenson's advice that cautious reconstruction of the Freetown City Council was "the most expedient step in the direction of self-government";[46] here at least it seemed possible to control the application of Williams's "tentative plan". But Stevenson's conservatism encountered more resolute opposition than expected; Freetonians refused to register to elect what they feared would be another subordinate municipality, and consequently any consideration of reconstituting the legislature was delayed. This delay was possibly more welcome than otherwise to officials with urgent priorities elsewhere, but the result was that the programme of political education envisaged for phase one provided largely abortive.[47]

THE LABOUR GOVERNMENT IN THE POST-WAR WORLD

The transfer of power in West Africa thus ranked low among the priorities of Colonial Office "forward thinking", even at the end of the war. Constitutional reform was largely an addition to a "planned policy" centred on the theme of development, and had been brought forward by Governors more sensitive than Whitehall to the changing tone of African opinion. It was hoped that reformed institutions would provide a framework for co-operation with a wider spectrum of African leadership, embracing trade unionists and other spokesmen for the commoners as well as the traditional intermediary elites; and that this might secure not merely the "acquiescence" of Africans but their active acceptance of the new goals of colonial policy. The new catch-phrase of "partnership" (another word for collaboration) was intended to apply in West Africa as well as in the colonies with settler minorities, and "harmony of the black and white keys" seemed a long-term necessity.[48] (Even such harmony involved a shift in attitudes which not all officials found it easy to make; the new Nigerian constitution would have had a better start had Richards shown the same readiness to consult as Burns.)

But it became increasingly clear that only on new political foundations could the resources of the colonial empire be used to restore Britain's battered strategic and economic interests in the post-war world. It is arguable that the importance of the West African colonies to the United Kingdom had become greater than ever before. West Africa was a prolific source of raw materials and foodstuffs, with dollar-earning cocoa as one of the sterling area's few immediate assets; and new routes of international communications developed during the war had enhanced the strategic importance of its harbours and airfields. But Britain's diminished resources, and her appreciation of the colonial contribution to victory, meant that these imperial purposes would have to be served within new collaborative frameworks where the power of initiative would be more evenly shared between metropolis and periphery.

In Eastern Africa (which always played a more important role than the West in Imperial strategy) such a framework seemed in the 1940s to depend upon inter-racial power-sharing with built-in European leadership, and upon inter-colonial co-operation to ensure stronger blocks of power.[49] Traces of both ideas can be found in the West African files; also, for example in the Colonial Office desire to perpetuate the inter-territorial organization of the Resident Minister in a West African Council, where a British Minister with a strong and independent secretariat would preside over the periodic Governors' meetings.[50] As noted above, there were also occasional flirtations with ideas of multi-racialism. But the Colonial Office, if not all the politicians, understood that "East Africa differs so much from West Africa, both as regards the state of political advancement of Africans and as regards the admixture of immigrant communities, that only on the very broadest of principles is anything done in West Africa likely to affect East Africa".[51] Whereas in the East it was feasible to regard Europeans as the long-term collaborators of Empire, hoping for some future Capricornian Smuts, in West Africa, (as in Asia) there would eventually be only the indigenous peoples. Hence the political changes somewhat timidly accepted during the war, together with the programmes for African advancement, economic development and social improvement, became crucial means of ensuring West African collaboration in Britain's last attempts to maintain an imperial role in the world of super-powers.

Recent studies of British political history tend to diminish the historical significance of the Labour electoral victory of 1945 (which the writer, like many of his contemporaries, hailed as the start of a new political era). Dr Paul Addison's masterly study presents the Attlee government as heir to "a broad agenda of safe and constructive progress",[52] adumbrated during the miseries of the 1930s, but given practical form under urgent wartime pressures. While the essential political framework was provided by the Coalition, Dr Addison perceives the solid content of this new reforming consensus as originating in the new commitment to planning of civil servants, increasingly allied with academics and the emergent technocrats of the policy-making elite.

Dr Addison's book appears to contain only one passing reference to colonial policy: in 1943 Attlee, Bevin and Morrison included it in a list of subjects suitable for consensual decision.[53] But his general thesis seems eminently applicable; Hailey could well have appeared in his book as the Beveridge of the colonial empire. While the 1945 election certainly gave office to men whose professions of faith (unlike those of some of their opponents) firmly committed them to new approaches, the general course had already been mapped in a bi-partisan or non-partisan atmosphere around Whitehall, under the political and economic impulses of depression and war. George Hall, Attlee's first Secretary of State, had served his colonial apprenticeship under Moyne, Cranborne and Stanley; since he seems to have preferred to do business orally rather than on paper, his personal influence is hard to trace but it does not seem to have been profound. Arthur Creech Jones, who succeeded him late in 1946, is a more significant figure, not least because his long-standing concern to investigate African grievances which were brought to his notice, and his role in the Fabian Colonial Bureau since 1940, had earned him good expectations among African leaders. Rather than a political innovator, Creech Jones was a sincere colonial reformer co-opted into the policy-making elite (as a member of the Advisory

Committee on Education in the Colonies since 1936, as Vice-Chairman of the Elliot Committee); his absorption in the details of worthy projects may sometimes have blinded him to wider issues.[54] In December 1946 he addressed to a meeting of the Fabian Colonial Bureau an extensive "profession of faith" under the title "Labour's Colonial Policy"; virtually every innovation there mentioned could be shown to have orginated in the Colonial Office under the wartime Coalition.[55] This does not mean that the radical and Socialist writers from whom the Fabians claimed descent had counted for nothing: rather, that the reforming conscience had been co-opted to support a new colonial consensus.

Revisionism need not go so far as to suggest that the Labour victory had no importance for Africa. Apart from reinforcing such specific reforms as those designed to encourage a "responsible" trade union leadership, it ensured that the new Development and Welfare Act would be applied under a Parliament more sensitive to African needs and aspirations than its Conservative-dominated predecessor might have been. But as Low and Lonsdale point out, the indirect institutional effects of that Act were arguably more important than its direct financial contribution. While the technical capacity of the Colonial Office itself to intervene was being vastly enlarged, colonial governments too were encouraged to draw up long-term plans (or shopping lists); when funds available from London proved disappointing, but revenue from export crops and the new income-tax proved buoyant, they could now choose to finance development locally. But the execution of such plans (however financed) produced a "second colonial occupation" in the form of a large-scale infusion of technical experts, whose activities not only increased the "intensity" of colonial government, but seemed to imply its continuance in some form until the new policies had an opportunity to mature. Ardent Socialists were among the warmest supporters of this technocratic approach: Ian Mikardo, in a Fabian pamphlet of 1948 entitled *The Second Five Years*, gave pride of place to "joint British-French-Belgian-South African-Egyptian planning and development of the greater part of Africa". The imperatives of domestic reconstruction could lead colonial reformers to press colonial development schemes (as for Tanganyikan groundnuts) without carefully calculating those benefits to Africans which their rhetoric assumed to be the real justification for development.

There is a related aspect of this "second occupation" which Low and Lonsdale hardly mention. Some of the specialists who carried out the second occupation were themselves convinced radicals or Socialists, who believed that the transfer of their own particular expertise, knowledge and working values, to African successors was an essential part of that wider transfer of power to which they saw themselves committed. The following chapter of this book describes how Edgar Parry in Sierra Leone "discovered" Siaka Stevens as a man capable, not only of guiding the embryonic trade union movement along soundly constitutional lines, but of leading a wider social democratic movement "with its hooks well into both sides of Transport House". But it was perhaps the educationalists, moving out to teach in the Elliot University colleges and elsewhere, who best exemplify this urge to form successors in their own image. Thomas Hodgkin, persuading the Colonial Office in 1946 to sponsor an extension to West Africa of the political education offered by the Oxford Extra-Mural Delegacy, provides an example of radical neo-colonialism which even the strongest anti-imperialist must applaud.[56] It would be interesting to estimate the effects of the classes which grew out of this visit on the developing ideas and objectives of African political leaders.

Even radical decolonizers still expected the preparatory period of partnership to be lengthy; nobody knew better than a specialist how long the economic and social foundations of nationhood would take to lay. Plans were being initiated which would take decades to mature fully; it seemed desirable to most experts, and feasible to the officials, to govern the timing of political transfer accordingly. Ronald Robinson has argued [57] that the memoranda prepared for discussion by the African Governors' Conference of November 1947 by an official Committee under Sir Sidney Caine gave a new priority to political and constitutional change. Unlike Williams's "tentative plan" of 1943, these gave detailed attention to processes by which executive authority might be partially transferred into African hands, breathed urgency into the policy of reconstructing the foundations of local government, and sought to relate political change to programmes of social and economic development. As officials became aware of rising African expectations they thus sought to anticipate them in order to retain the political initiative. Yet Cohen still assumed that, even in the Gold Coast, "internal self-Government is unlikely to be achieved in much less than a generation"; and any further acceleration of the time-table was bound to upset newly-calculated relationships between social and economic advance and "the slow work of nation-building". Only within limits could one accelerate the capacity of new universities to train highly sophisticated cadres, or the implementation of carefully balanced proposals for improved patterns of land use. At *some* stage further acceleration of constitutional development would involve qualitative change in the whole concept of planned preparation for the transfer of power.

The need to accelerate came much sooner than Cohen could have expected. From late 1947, after Burns's departure, unrest in the Gold Coast intensified; inflationary pressures produced a well organised boycott of high-priced European manufactures, and in the countryside cocoa-farmers protested against government measures to enforce the "cutting-out" of diseased trees. The United Gold Coast Convention, led by its new General Secretary Kwame Nkrumah, used these and other grievances to organize support. On 28 February 1948 a demonstration by ex-servicemen in Accra was fired on by police, who killed two men and wounded four or five; three days of rioting followed, extending from Accra to other towns, including Kumasi. Governor Creasy declared a state of emergency and Nkrumah appealed for international support by telegrams to assorted recipients in New York, London and Moscow. But by 4 March the country seems to have been relatively calm. Total casualties (including three killed and four injured during revived outbreaks in Kumasi on 15–18 March) were officially estimated at 29 dead and 237 injured.[58] In the context of imperial history, this hardly seems a major crisis; one may speculate whether a more experienced and resolute Governor, confident of the support of police and officials, might not have contained the situation locally. But the magnitude of the consequences far exceeded that of the events themselves; these riots led directly towards Ghanaian independence nine years later.

Part of the explanation may be found in the international background. 1948, which would prove a year of destiny for the Commonwealth in Africa, saw the climax of the Cold War. The Communist seizure of power in Prague earlier in February had converted many liberals and Social Democrats to the thesis that the Communists were driving towards world mastery; in June such fears were reinforced by the Berlin blockade. Mao Tse-tung's decisive offensive was about to begin; during this same month of February Asian Communist youth movements were conferring in Calcutta, and by June the grumbling disorders in Malaya would reach the status of "emergency".[59] Maladroit British responses to the inconclusive evidence of Nkrumah's Communism must be understood in this alarming context.[60] We still have little direct evidence about military influence on colonial policy, but the general climate nourished broad concepts of world strategy, worked out upon small maps. In November 1948 the Chief of Imperial General Staff could solemnly harangue African Legislative Councillors about the need for a "Master Plan" to contain Communism by a union of African territories under "the great dominion in the south";[61] more sober appraisals must have suggested that a more realistic policy would be closer collaboration with an authentic West African leadership capable of resisting Communist blandishments.

In 1948, that seemed to exclude Nkrumah. Even those who discounted his Communist affiliations must have seen the danger to established economic interests and social relationships in a leader who by appealing so effectively not only to new sections of the urban population but to discontented rural commoners, threatened to bridge the "enormous gulf" which Williams had used in 1943 to justify a measured pace of constitutional reform. How far British policy-makers drew direct analogies with India, recognizing in the militant cocoa-farmers a class of "dominant peasants" like those who had provided Congress with so much support, we do not yet know.[62] But the riots did provide a clear warning that, unless the British broadened the basis of their rule in West Africa, sooner or later they would be faced with something worse. It was not an isolated crisis; the Lagos strike of 1945, though less violent, had been potentially more serious. An even graver situation might well have developed in Nigeria after the Enugu shooting of November 1949, had Sir Hugh Foot not by then begun to recover the all-important "initiative";[63] and in that vast and complex country it would have been harder to improvise a technique of controlled transfer of power. Although the Gold Coast was no straightforward case, it did seem to provide enough of the supposed preconditions for self-government to make acceleration of the constitutional time-table an acceptable gamble.[64]

The Watson Commission had made specific proposals for constitutional reform; but later in 1948 the Government remitted these to a committee of forty African notables under Justice Coussey. This was a bold and imaginative attempt to reconstruct the system of collaboration within a traditional Gold Coast framework of "chiefs and intellectuals", and so invalidate Nkrumah's claim to speak for those African masses whose interests never lacked self-appointed defenders. The British Cabinet, now convinced "that in the present state of political development in the Gold Coast no system would be workable which did not provide for a very considerable degree of African participation in the control of policy",[65] approved the apparently far-reaching Coussey proposals, but with one major qualification. By rejecting as premature the idea of an embryonic prime minister who would nominate Africans for appointment to the Executive Council, they in effect denied that any African political party could yet bridge the gap between the aspirations of rural Africans and the political rituals of Accra: they had learned the lesson which Namier was teaching from British history, that until the advent of "strongly organized, disciplined parliamentary parties" the sovereign retained the initiative in appointing ministers.[66] But Nkrumah too must have included some history in his spasmodic studies at LSE; success in the Colony elections of February 1951 marked a temporary capture of the initiative by his Convention Peoples' Party. Sir Charles Arden-Clarke could recover it in part only by recognizing the necessity of accepting those collaborators whom the electorate had designated, and hoping that six-year transitional period would permit the transfer of objectives and values, as well as of power, to African successors. Efforts, as Creech Jones put it, had to be made "to direct new forces into constructive channels".[67] By 1957 there was some guarded official optimism that the Ghanaian regime to which power was being transferred would maintain some at least of its predecessor's constructive policies, domestically and within the Commonwealth.

Though the social and ethnic diversity of Nigeria made the transfer of power in Lagos a more complex operation, that very complexity gave the colonial government certain opportunities of initiative. Although the Colonial Office had rejected the separatism favoured by some Northern administrators, it still seemed possible – even necessary – to use the weight of the conservative North to restrain the ambitions of Southern politicians. But Richards's maladroit handling of his constitutional proposals, together with the social pressures revealed by the Lagos strike of 1945, showed that there were deep sources of discontent in the South and that it was important to regain the confidence of the leaders. Here the manifest sincerity of Hugh Foot, Chief Secretary from 1947 to 1951, was an undoubted asset. By sponsoring widely-based committees to examine the sensitive questions of constitutional revision and Africanization of the public service, the government of Nigeria avoided such losses of initiative as had occurred in the Gold Coast in 1948 and 1951. The improvements in prices for primary products after the Korean War, accentuating the general improvement in barter terms of trade between 1945 and 1960, also helped to blunt the political radicalism which had begun to seem menacing during the later 1940s.[68]

Once the process of constitutional revision had been re-opened, the pressure of events in the Gold Coast alone was sufficient to ensure an accelerating momentum in Nigeria. The Southern leaders would not be satisfied with less than their Ghanaian brothers; Northern conservatives increasingly saw the necessity, and the tangible advantages, of joining in. But the tempo of political transfer at the centre left no opportunity to reconsider the unwidely tri-regional structure on which successive constitutions rested. The decolonizers could only work through those specific groups of leaders who had emerged within the old administrative regions; and in varying degrees the NCNC, the Action Group, and the Northern Peoples' Congress came to be regarded as controlled by Igbos, Yorubas, and conservative Muslim aristocrats respectively. Not only Hailey and Bourdillon but Azikiwe and Awolowo had suggested that the regional pattern required reconstruction; but, quite apart from the NPC's interest in maintaining a monolithic North, there simply was not time for this. The Willink Commission of 1958 was instructed to assume the existence of "Minorities", and to seek means of allaying their fears; though authorized to recommend the creation of new states "as a last resort", they were in no doubt that the consequent delay in the transfer of power would be as unwelcome to the Macmillan government as to Nigerian leaders. Their elegant application to the Nigerian federation of Western liberal-democratic doctrines, re-read in light of the Nigerian civil war, seems essentially a justification of the politically unavoidable.[69]

Although during the Second World War the Colonial Office repeatedly asserted that the four West African territories would have to be treated individually in light of such criteria as "viability" or "readiness for self-government", it soon became clear that there would be no attempt to retain Sierra Leone and The Gambia once Ghana and Nigeria were independent. Despite the Committee on Smaller Territories which the Colonial Office established during the later 1940s, events in Sierra Leone at least were now shaped by reactions on the periphery rather than debates at the centre of Empire. In 1951 the political deadlock created in Freetown by the intransigent particularism of the Creole National Council was broken by Governor Beresford-Stooke, who after the election took the first decisive steps towards a transfer of executive responsibility to the elected leaders of the Sierra Leone Peoples' Party. Though their political influence rested largely on very imperfectly modernized chieftaincies, they now were the only credible "collaborators" in sight. The incipient diamond boom, besides increasing the political stakes, provided some short-term answers to questions about "vaiability". (Only today, as Sierra Leone's mineral resources threaten to run out, is the full significance of that concept about to be tested.) The Gambia's minute size seemed to raise graver problems, and for a time there was even some discussions of integration with Britain; but since metropolitan wisdom could devise no politically acceptable alternative, independence came here too in 1964, and has so far proved more "viable" than in many larger and richer states.

The argument of this chapter may now be summarized. During the Second World War the transfer of political power to West African hands, formerly a vague aspiration for an indefinite future, was specifically envisaged as the culmination of comprehensive programmes of social engineering, designed to reconstruct African societies to accord with the ideas and interests of a changing British Commonwealth. But pressures from within Africa, and from the changing balance of international power, radically modified these intentions; although the Colonial Office had much success in retaining the tactical initiative, this meant reversing the priorities of their strategy. They moved from a policy of subordinating controlled constitutional experiment to programmes of social and economic developments, through a phase of "nation-building" and accelerated preparation for self-government, into conditions where the speedy transfer of power to acceptable African collaborators became an end in itself. The British government, genuinely converted during the 1930s by the colonial reformers, ended by discovering that the political objective of the anti-imperialists was more in accordance with the economic and strategic realities of their diminished position in the world.

Tactical flexibility enabled the British largely to determine the institutional framework within which radical African leaders like

Nkrumah and Azikiwe agreed to collaborate in the transfer of power. In the process of collaboration the radicalism of some of these leaders, perhaps never very deeply grounded, became attenuated or corrupted – sometimes by material temptations, sometimes by the prospects of influence within the political contexts of Commonwealth or United Nations, sometimes perhaps by simple despair at discovering discrepancies (already well known to colonial governments) between constitutional responsibility and effective power. Few historians would dare to predict the fortunes of any African state over the next quarter-century; but they are likely to differ from the versions of pan-African ideologues almost as much as from officially-sponsored plans for the post-colonial order.

3 Approaches to Decolonization in Sierra Leone

To understand the past involves two very different operations, and to synthesize them is a severe test of historical scholarship. On the one hand historians study change over an extended period of time, and try to discern in what underlying direction the twisting course of events was leading; at the same time they must immerse themselves in the detailed evidence for those events, seeking to do justice to the thoughts and purposes of men whose own conceptions of what they were doing, and where they were going, may now seem to have been ironically mistaken. Both operations present peculiar difficulties in studying events so near in time, and so contentious, as the termination of colonial rule in Africa.

In the long perspective of history, the period when Europeans exercised direct political control over West African peoples was brief: except in a few special areas closely involved in the conduct of oceanic trade, it nowhere exceeded the life-time of an old man. But were these years of revolutionary importance? Jacob Ajayi regards the colonial period as "just another episode . . . in the continuous flow of African history":[1] Africans who successfully practised the "politics of survival" were able eventually to recover their sovereignty with their essential identities intact, having acquired new institutions, techniques and problems without suffering fundamental social or cultural upheaval. He could find unwanted support among those old imperialists who, shaking their heads over the latest news from Uganda or Angola, conclude that Africans are reverting to their unregenerate past; being colonized has done them no good at all.

Equally unnatural allies believe the colonial interlude to have been crucially important; apologists of empire join hands with radical theorists of neo-colonialism in their belief that the purpose and effect of colonial rule was to change the structure and the values of the colonized society into shapes more congruent with those of the imperial power. Both see colonial empire as something which was historically destined to wither away, once it had completed the "double mission" which Marx had foreseen for British rule in India: "the annihilation of old Asiatic society, and the laying of the material foundations of Western Society". Nowadays historians often describe the early nineteenth century as a period of "informal empire", when Britain in particular enjoyed many of the perquisites of power in Africa without the responsibilities of rule, hoping that acceptable forms of civilization would develop through moral suasion in church, school and market-place. After the partition military force reinforced this suasion, and other forms of power, based upon science and technology, were incorporated into colonial structures. But (so a speculative hypothesis might continue) this superiority of power could not be expected to last forever. Might not far-sighted colonial masters then seek to encourage a new "collaborating class", trained to use the weapons of the modern state as well as the sword of the spirit? If power was transferered into the right hands, could their successors not hope once more to enjoy the perquisites without the responsibilities?

Publicly proclaimed purposes of both French and British colonial empires do appear to support the view that these were destined ultimately to be self-liquidating, though in different ways. In French official theory, the end of empire would come, not with the restoration of self-government, but with its transformation into a sort of cosmopolitan super-state, through the gradual entry of individuals who had undergone a thorough cultural conversion into full political equality. Behind this astonishing vision lay assumptions so large that they may seem to rest on either naive innocence or conscious hypocrisy. Psychologically, assimilation implies conditioning individuals so completely that their own cultural inheritance becomes irrelevant – a possibility which enthusiasts found easier to assume for Black Africans than for Vietnamese or Arabs. Politically, the theory assumed the willingness of native Frenchmen to share power in the bureaucracy, the church, the teaching profession, as well as in the Assembly, with foreigners who would eventually greatly out-number them. And economically, it assumed an absence of fundamental conflict between rulers and subjects – a projection of the famous "harmony of interests". Even those who could accept such assumptions could hardly envisage a realization of the assimilationist ideal in their own life-times. Token gestures in this direction were the most that could be expected; until the Second World War at least assimilation was as irrelevant to the everyday concerns of the French administrator in Africa as was self-government to his British colleagues. Even the Brazzaville manifesto of 1944, when Republican colonial adminstrators committed themselves to reforms first propounded under the Popular Front, envisaged no early liquidation of Empire; but it provided sufficient evidence of good intentions to win the collaboration of authentic African leaders in its programme. This collaboration was in general maintained when the international pressures of the 1950s obliged France sharply to reverse her tactics, accepting African independence within a general framework of unequal power.

For the British, the post-war crises of Empire entailed no such revolution of principles. Statements of intent to involve the peoples of the Empire, at appropriately different speeds, in a majestic "progress towards self-government", were frequently made by twentieth-century publicists and historians, and, less frequently, imprecisely endorsed by official statements, like that by Malcolm MacDonald of 7 December 1938. But as far as Black Africa was concerned, what Kenneth Robinson calls "the tranquil assumption of the long-term character of colonial rule" was still almost universally accepted. This was true, not only of officials in Whitehall and Africa, but of that somewhat wider circle of politicians, academics, merchants and missionaries which constituted the "policy-making elite" of the 1930s and 1940s, and embraced even contemporary radical critics of imperialism.[2] When during the Second World War Americans and other foreigners began to interest themselves in these matters, it emerged that the statements of intent had made little impact upon what administrators actually did; Churchill's declaration of September 1941 that unambiguous commitments already guaranteed "the progressive evolution of self-governing institutions" in each colony could not be substantiated from the record.

By this time the assumptions of British colonial policy were changing; just as wartime vicissitudes led the French to re-assess their policies at Brazzaville, so Churchill's statement reflected growing acceptance of eventual political decolonization. The general lines along which colonial policy evolved have been sketched in Chapter 2; this chapter attempts to trace their faltering search for new "collaborators" in Sierra Leone, a colony of potential strategic value, where internal African pressures were less insistent and independence was less clearly an inevitable, or indeed an attainable, goal. "It would be obviously absurd to think of all the existing Colonial units as being equally fit for self-government," wrote O. G. Williams in 1943;[3] no doubt the exiguous territorial, economic and demographic resources of The Gambia were uppermost in his mind, but Sierra Leone, with a population of under two million and a far from impressive economy, was until many years later commonly regarded as a marginal case from the point of view of the elusive and rarely defined quality of "viability". This uncertainty was increased by the doubts which many Britons felt about an established elite which comprised the oldest group of "collaborators" in British West Africa – the Creoles. Though a less crucial case than Nigeria or the Gold Coast, Sierra Leone offers interesting opportunities for studying the contradictions and hesitancies of British policy during this period of change.

THE REJECTION OF THE CREOLES

During much of the nineteenth century the Colony of Sierra Leone (that is, Freetown and its satellite settlements) became the home of an African population profoundly influenced by those modernizing and Westernizing forces which Victorians summarized as "Christianity, civilization and commerce". Although these settlers and recaptives proved less culturally malleable than some expected, fusing African and European elements into a distinctive Creole synthesis,[4] their political spokesmen assumed that the new African nation which they aspired to lead would be decisively influenced by Anglo-Saxon attitudes of church, school and market-place, and would freely collaborate with the British Empire. They saw themselves, and were seen by others, as heirs-apparent of the British.

Unfortunately, even before the imperialist impulse of the 1890s brought the expansion of British control over the Protectorate, British officials had abandoned these optimistic assumptions. Racially-minded authoritarians and benevolent paternalists shared low expectations of Creole capacity, and no longer contemplated that transfer of administration which a Parliamentary Committee had envisaged in 1865. The initial successes of Sierra Leoneans in expanding the commercial frontiers of British capitalism were not sustained; African churches ceased to seem relevant to self-government; the schools of the missionaries were reshaped on lines

Approaches to Decolonization in Sierra Leone 53

more consistent with scientific imperialism. Although institutions like Fourah Bay College continued to provide colonial West Africa with an indispensable supply of public servants, these worthy men were no longer regarded as political heirs. The immediately permissible limit of self-government was indicated by the emasculated Freetown Municipality created in 1893; conceived less as a seed-bed of liberty than as a method of developing financial responsibility, this body never inspired much confidence among Africans or Europeans. When it was suspended in 1926 under the shadow of financial irregularities, there was no strong call to replace it. Victorian Britain's model African colony had broken down.

But had the British genuinely sought to prepare a "collaborating class" to carry on the work of Empire in West Africa by other means, the Creoles, with their strong attachment to British political, constitutional and legal values, would still have had much to commend them. It is true that the generation represented by the National Congress of British West Africa, still strident with resentment at their rejection by the new imperialism, did not look very promising as *interlocuteurs valables* for a Sierra Leonean nation;[5] H. C. Bankole Bright, the leading elected member of the Legislative Council from 1924 to 1939, was noted chiefly for an oratorical style as ostentatiously out-dated and inappropriate as his Edwardian businessman's costume. Yet myopic Governors did not use their powers of patronage to encourage alternative leaders; Governor Douglas Jardine, re-nominating the worthy barrister C. E. Wright for a fourth term on the Council, claimed that no other suitable candidates were available.[6] Many of Wright's most distinguished contemporaries were of course in government service, but Jardine's own successor thought this ought not to be incompatible with membership of the Legislative Council; in any case the decline of civic virtue among the Creoles was certainly not so complete as their critics claimed. Their leaders still coloured their concern to revive and liberalize this stagnant dependency with fervent Empire loyalism. As the weekly *West Africa* was to say at the end of the war:

> To a London official headquarters endowed with a little imagination, it might occur to develop this feeling, as a precious link with Britain, and an advertisement of recent loudly-proclaimed intentions to develop every form of local government in the dependencies.[7]

Yet nobody loved the Creoles. The young Graham Greene reacted to his first sight of Freetown by a blistering satire, which he later admitted was misdirected.[8] Jardine, in a curious phrase, confessed almost shame-facedly to a "sneaking regard" for this community, yet regarded their political claims as "rooted in sentiment rather than reason".[9] Arthur Dawe, responsible for West African affairs as Assistant Under-Secretary in the Colonial Office from 1938 to 1945, who had been Secretary to the 1926 enquiry into the Freetown municipality, regarded Creoles as "a specially inflammable breed", to whom only restricted liberties could be permitted.[10] Such attitudes seem to reflect an instinctive rejection of black men who might appear to parody attitudes and ideologies of Englishmen; but underlying them was an appreciation of social and cultural differences between Creoles and the indigenous peoples of the Protectorate. For even in the twentieth century the Creoles remained a favoured community – not only enjoying superior (though strictly circumscribed) opportunities for subordinate office, honour and emolument within colonial society, but absorbing a proportionately high share of government expenditure on schools, medical services and economic infrastructure. British administrators perpetuated these distinctions even as they deplored them, hesitating to disturb the tranquil stagnation of the provinces so long as peace could be maintained.[11] During the 1930s islands of social change had begun to appear in the Protectorate, largely as a result of mining developments; internal and external movements of people were intensified and Colony and Protectorate gradually drawn into closer relationships.[12] But in Sierra Leone as elsewhere, the Colonial Office hoped to control the new problems by the paternal sponsorship of new social and economic policies; politically, they maintained the policy introduced in 1936, of trying to apply the classical principles of indirect rule to the small chiefdoms of the Protectorate. When in 1938 a new Creole-based political movement began to challenge this approach, official hostility intensified.

THE RISE OF THE YOUTH LEAGUE

The West African Youth League, a political movement which has recently attracted scholarly attention, was largely the creation of I. T. A. Wallace-Johnson, a critic of colonialism who remains difficult to evaluate.[13] He was clearly eloquent, courageous, and very ingenious in exploiting the circumscribed freedoms permitted by British colonial rule; yet in retrospect his career seems lacking in consistency and integrity of purpose. Although "liberty or Death" was a fine slogan – and Wallace-Johnson suffered severely in the cause of extending freedom of speech and publication – it was never very clear what *use* Africans were to make of their liberty; as Dr Kaniki observes, the Youth League never demanded independence, and the thrust of its radicalism remained indiscriminate and diffuse. The writer's recollection of Wallace-Johnson in his late fifties is of a self-indulgent opportunist, yoked with the most conservative of his former opponents; both opportunism and self-indulgence seem to be foreshadowed in the charismatic hero of 1938–9.

Wallace-Johnson returned to Sierra Leone as a known associate of Communists, and no doubt it was this which led Customs officers to publicize his arrival in April 1938 by seizing copies of the *African Sentinel*. But it is doubtful whether he remained in any sense a Communist;[14] his basic philosophy was a somewhat diffusely radical pan-Africanism similar to that of his mentor George Padmore – whom Johnson used to address in the name of "my sainted grandfather, Jaja of Opobo".[15] His reputation did not prevent the intelligent Colonial Secretary, Hilary Blood, from expressing the opinion (late abandoned) that "the way to neutralize his effect was to appoint him to the Legislative Council";[16] the intense official hostility which soon developed seems to have been due less to the Youth League's specific ideas or programme than to its fiercely independent attitude, and its apparent success in exploiting forces of racial antagonism which Jardine perceived latent within the frustrated constitutionalism of the Creoles.[17]

More dangerous still to the policy of controlled paternalism: the Youth League's cosmopolitan approach to the problems of Sierra Leone not only won enthusiastic support among Creoles (who repeatedly packed meetings at the Wilberforce Hall through 1938, and patronized the *frondeur* journalism of Wallace-Johnson's *African Standard*) but threatened to affect the Protectorate-born proletariat, both in Freetown and in the mining locations. After Wallace-Johnson made a provincial tour in July 1938 (not including the gold and diamond areas) the League claimed branches in Bo, Moyamba, Bonthe, Mano, Lunsar and Pepel. These may have consisted largely of Creoles, and Dr Kaniki is inclined to qualify W. M. Macmillan's contemporary conclusion that "the ventilation of constitutional or labour grievances has begun to bridge the deep cleavage between the Creoles and the peoples of the Protectorate";[18] but the provincial administration was embarrassed by the emergence of an organization capable of observing and politicizing the errors and excesses of its agents. Thus the League took up the claims of residents in Bonthe, whose houses had been irregularly demolished by officials over-zealous for the cause of sanitation;[19] more alarmingly, their investigations of irregularities and cruelties during the collection of house-tax stimulated Parliamentary questions and press publicity in Britain which provided material for Nazi propaganda. The colonial government, stirred to make its own enquiries, discovered that there had indeed been "acts of gross brutality" by Court Messengers, and that one reluctant tax-payer had been flogged to death.[20]

Jardine was quick to apprehend that Wallace-Johnson might succeed in mobilizing the growing proletariat to threaten colonial authority; "in the event of a strike at one of the mines he would be a potential danger to the peace and good order of the country," he wrote on 30 June 1938.[21] Events during the next year increased these fears. Some, like Jardine's abortive attempt to prosecute the Youth League for a breach of official secrecy,[22] enabled Wallace-Johnson to score points against the government within the recognized rules of colonial constitutionality; others, like the strikes of labourers in Freetown in January 1939 and of iron-miners at Marampa in May, held more alarming implications. Real grievances over wages and working conditions underlay these strikes, and the Provincial Commissioner rejected the temptation to blame the trouble at Marampa on "external agitators";[23] but it was Wallace-Johnson who had provided the impetus for the formation of trade unions, and for a pitiful little "strike" by Army recruits in January 1939.

Colonial officials thus reacted with almost visceral hostility to the political pretensions of the Youth League, even when they recognized that the conditions it was denouncing required reform; Jardine had to be discreetly warned by the Colonial Office "to get off his high horse and to remember that you can't do the 'Sanders of the River' stuff in Freetown".[24] Even Blood abandoned hope of collaborating with Wallace-Johnson, and contemplated deporting him.[25] He remained, he said "anxious . . . to get the Youth League on the side of Government or at any rate to recognize it as an organization whom we can meet and with whom we can treat, but I see no chance of doing this so long as Johnson is Organizing

Secretary".[26] Jardine's wilder suggestions of abridging the right of election were ruled out by the Colonial Office, but widespread Creole hostility was still aroused by four Ordinances designed to control the activities of the Youth League, and safeguard the security of Freetown as a defended port, which he was allowed to enact in June 1939; these provided for the more expeditious trial and punishment of persons accused of sedition, or of inciting troops to disobedience; for the tighter control of imported publications; and for the preventive detention of "undesirable British subjects".[27]

This fortification of colonial authority was however accompanied by attempts to redress social grievances. The same session of the Legislative Council passed other Ordinances which legalized registered trade unions, authorized peaceful picketing, provided for government-sponsored processes of arbitration and enquiry, and introduced the principle of workman's compensation; and when a newly-appointed Labour Secretary took up his duties in July he soon began to secure co-operation from the eight rudimentary unions which Wallace-Johnson had brought into existence.[28] With the outbreak of war jobs became plentiful in Freetown, on defence works and in providing supplies and services to ships assembling in the harbour; and although this activity was clearly generating social problems for the future,[29] the political thrust of the Youth League was blunted when Wallace-Johnson was interned under wartime emergency powers. The war brought out the Empire loyalism of the Creole bourgeoisie, and the continuing sniping of the *African Standard* does not seem to have struck very deeply.

THE ABORTING OF "STAGE ONE"

With the threat from the Youth League apparently overcome, Hailey's report on political development provided little stimulus to prepare for decolonization in Sierra Leone. A short visit to Freetown in March 1940 led Hailey to embrace the official wisdom concerning the essential irresponsibility of the Creole community. "Their attachment to European institutions is unfortunately not supported by their economic situation and their apparent capacity for improving it," his report asserted; the success of the Youth League showed how easily Creoles could be "swept away by movements led by persons with low standards of responsibility and lacking in any sense of political restraint".[30] Even in Freetown, formerly regarded as their "sphere of civic usefulness",[31] Hailey judged it impossible to restore the powers of the municipality, given the Creole record and the continuing growth of the non-Creole population.[32] It followed that the "political development" of Sierra Leone would have to be regulated by change in the Protectorate.

Such a view virtually excluded for generations any dilution of the powers of the Governor; for though Hailey's report on the recently introduced system of native administration was framed in encouraging tones, it revealed only the most rudimentary capacity to administer the affairs of a modern state.[33] By 1941, 73 out of 216 chiefdoms had been reorganized; but with an average population of under 10 000 and correspondingly low taxable capacity, they had little opportunity to demonstrate their political responsibility. With the fruits of reorganization visible chiefly in the form of personal emoluments for individuals, of reconstructed prisons and courthouses, the new system was unlikely to inspire popular enthusiasm, or to inspire "the young men element" to play the civic roles for which Hailey hoped. Nor were administrators anxious to encourage such possibly troublesome elements. Blood hoped that eventually the government would "be able to point to the success of the NAs as what can be done by people who are regarded by the intelligentsia of Freetown as still being in the same almost savage state",[34] and many Mendes and Temnes were indeed already capable of political leadership. But most of them were employed by the government, which did nothing to permit their participation, and envisaged only the admission to the NAs of "progressive elements of those groups which by custom have the right to be represented".[35] This patronizing approach to the reform of local institutions from the grass roots up never inspired sustained enthusiasm from "progressive elements" in any African country; it certainly could not do so in Sierra Leone. Even if the NAs did make progress with road-building, with providing dispensaries and schools, such local initiatives could make little impact upon the total problems of poverty, disease and illiteracy unless accompanied by increased provision of services and skilled personnel by the central government.

The Colonial Development and Welfare Act of 1940 offered some possibility of financial support for accelerating these essential preparations for self-government – for example, the expansion of

Western education, without which many Native Authorities would be quite incapable of supervising even the limited programmes envisaged.[36] Yet in Sierra Leone the resources provided by the Act were not effectively deployed to support any clear political strategy. Harassed officials responded to the new opportunities offered by Whitehall in dilatory and piecemeal ways. Their reluctance to undertake constructive long-term planning was reflected in alarm when the Colonial Office suggested using the war as an opportunity to introduce income-tax. Jardine resisted this on three grounds; that it was not fiscally necessary, that it would weaken African systems of providing for the sick and poor through family structures and voluntary associations, and that – given the long history of Creole resistance to direct taxation – it would incite opposition and fortify the Youth League in demanding constitutional reform. But the Colonial Office persisted, thinking that Jardine took "too conservative a view of the trend of social and economic progress in West Africa",[37] but insisting above all that the *principle* of direct taxation should be established during the war as a necessary administrative and financial foundation for post-war expansion. Eventually Cranborne over-ruled the objections of the Governors of Sierra Leone and the Gold Coast (where the record of political opposition was equally strong);[38] income-tax was introduced in 1943 and, as foreseen, became a leading political issue.

In addition to this general conservatism, there was a special difficulty in reconciling the Colonial Office "development policy" with the political assumptions of the Sierra Leone administration. Initially, at least, grants to provide more efficiently specialized services might well accentuate the country's lop-sided social and educational structures, for some at least of these would be spent in reinforcing the privileged position of the Creoles. In 1937, 60 per cent of all educational expenditure had been committed to the Colony;[39] the structures it provided, inadequate though they might be, would have to form the base of future development. When in December 1941 the Director of Education was invited to "prepare a programme of educational development" with CD & W funds, his hard-pressed Department took two years to produce a mere patchwork of requests for assistance "to ensure more rapid development on existing lines".[40] As the Colonial Office Advisory Committee commented, it was "solely a memorandum put forward for the improvement and development of the Education Department; but something more than this appears to be needed in Sierra

Leone".[41] Its first three items provided for rebuilding of Colony schools, scholarships for advanced study overseas (which inevitably went largely to well-qualified Creoles),[42] and the appointment of a classics tutor to Fourah Bay College.

Fourah Bay, that precarious symbol of past Creole eminence, exemplified this particular dilemma; to abandon it would be contrary to the whole new development policy, to expand it would in the short run reinforce the old foundations of Creole privilege. In 1938 an inspecting Commission had found the College making the best of an essentially unsatisfactory situation. Out of thirty-two students (twenty from Sierra Leone) only twelve were taking degree courses; a small staff had to make "hand-to-mouth" arrangements to meet very diverse commitments, a tiny library was "like the curriculum, examination ridden".[43] In 1942 the College, further depleted in numbers, was displaced from its Freetown site by defence needs and rehoused in unsuitable quarters at Mabang; it seemed hardly relevant to the Elliot Commission's bold design of training cadres for independent African states. Yet even Elliot and his advisers could not contemplate completely abandoning an institution which had done so much to educate earlier West African elites; under Creole and missionary leadership the College retained a steadily growing place in successive educational plans and eventually (almost despite the planners) grew into the national University of Sierra Leone.

The fruits of the Development and Welfare Act were thus accepted in Sierra Leone almost incidentally, and not related to the Colonial Office's emerging ideas of political change. Though those who benefited would within twenty years hold political, administrative and judicial offices in independent Sierra Leone, few local officials seem to have been conscious of engaging in the first stage of a programme of constitutional development. The gap between assumptions and expectations – between the perception of officials like Williams that changing world conditions made it necessary to "get down to formulating our constitutional policy for West Africa and also be planning a programme for carrying it out",[44] and their lack of confidence that much could be achieved with the human and material resources available in Sierra Leone – inhibited reform. Jardine's successor, Sir Hubert Stevenson, strongly resisted Burns's initiative in appointing Africans to the Executive Council, delayed following suit until March 1943 on somewhat specious grounds of military security, and made it clear to the Colonial Office that he regarded his ultimate compliance as a gesture of little positive value to Sierra Leone.[45]

During the autumn of 1943 Oliver Stanley, the new Secretary of State, toured West Africa, and in Nigeria and the Gold Coast held concrete discussions about constitutional changes. But as regards Sierra Leone Stanley seems to have set out with low expectations, and returned with them lower still. During preliminary discussions Stevenson had insisted that the gap between Creoles and Protectorate peoples precluded any rapid progress at the centre, and that the reconstruction of the Freetown City Council was "the most expedient step in the direction of self-government".[46] He had already appointed a Committee on this subject under A. C. C. Swayne, official president of the existing Council; its Report of 1944 formed the basis of a draft Bill prepared early in 1945.[47] Firstly the powers of the Council, recently extended to the provision of schools, were enlarged to include municipal housing, sanitation, and transport; the Report however emphasized that this ought not to involve any greater increase of rates than from the existing 2s 4d to 3s. Secondly, the Council was to have an elected majority: a mayor, three aldermen and nine councillors, as against seven nominated members. Three of these were intended to represent "labour interests"; this attempt to prevent a Creole monopoly in a city which during the war had acquired an increased majority of illiterate Protectorate immigrants was based on an enlightened concern to avoid fostering ethnic consciousness, by writing in separate representation for the different "Tribal Headmen".[48]

> The ideal to which we look forward [Swayne's Committee declared] is a Freetown of intelligent and independent citizens, not an agglomeration or even a federation of tribal detachments. The aim should be to instil a civic sense into the individual and to avoid any course which might perpetuate tribal consciousness. The Tribal Administrations of Freetown, we feel, may have their places as friendly societies and nurseries of sentiment alongside the Caledonian Societies, and Liverpool-Irish battalions, but not as an integral part of the local Government.

Other nominated members however were to represent government departments; their presence, together with provision for the colonial government to disallow appointments made by the Council, to supervise its finances, and if necessary take over its functions altogether, reflected the British concern "that in view of the important Imperial interests in the functioning of the port of Freetown, there should be adequate safeguards for efficient administration".[49] Moreover the Colonial Office, anxious to universalize the principle of multi-racialism, seems to have believed that even in the long run Europeans should have a role in the government of Freetown; one official at least defined the aim as "harmony of the black and white keys", with "black and white pulling together in a single team on a single job".[50]

Although the activities of European sailors and servicemen in wartime Freetown had inevitably produced inter-racial conflicts and friction, disturbing Jardine's vision of stable paternalist relations between rulers and ruled,[51] few Creoles rejected the principle of co-operation with Europeans; but they did expect a greater measure of control over their historic "province of Freedom" than these proposals envisaged, and municipal reform thus became the focus for a new consolidation of Creole political consciousness under the leadership of old Youth League militants. At first indeed the proposals were quite well received. The Notes of Dissent submitted by J. Fowell Boston, a Creole member of Swayne's Committee, centred on a proposal that civil servants should be eligible for election to the new Council; justified as a means of enlarging the pool of ability before the electorate, this seemed a possible channel for continuing indirect government control – and it was certainly notable that no such proposal was ever entertained in the Protectorate, where a far larger proportion of educated men were in government employment. But soon other reservations crept into public comment: some were based on the misapprehension that the aldermen would not need to secure election to the Council in the first place, some doubted the government's willingness to train Africans to serve as Town Clerk and Engineer, others suspected that the nominated "labour members" would be used by the government to curb Creole aspirations. Despite some concessions by the government, opposition to the Bill mounted; by January 1945 Boston was claiming the new Council would be "in effect a sub-department of government".[52]

The Government's olive-branch to the Creoles now became a provocation, with criticism increasingly centring on the reserve powers to be retained by the Governor. When Arthur Creech Jones became Under-Secretary in July 1945 he cited constitutional authorities like W. A. Robson to show that the Bill followed impeccable British precedents – always an important argument with the Creole Empire loyalists.[53] To this Thomas Decker replied that in the UK reserve powers were exercised by a government ultimately responsible to the electorate; municipal reform therefore should not precede reform of the Legislative Council but accompany it.[54] During 1945 the critics mobilized support for a boycott of the new Council; in August 1945 only one hundred and sixty applied to register as electors (compared to three thousand qualified under the old Ordinance) and it became clearly impossible to hold elections.[55]

Attempts to implement in Sierra Leone the first stage of the Colonial Office's "tentative plan for constitutional development"[56] were thus aborted. While the proposal municipal reform failed to satisfy Creole expectations, development in the Protectorate was proceeding slowly, and on lines which only confirmed their apprehension that the "backward" condition of the majority would be deliberately used to control the advance of the elite. In response to the thinking of London, plans were indeed made to establish advisory Councils in the twelve Districts, with a Protectorate Assembly largely elected through them; but these bodies would be composed almost exclusively of chiefs and representatives of Tribal Authorities who could be expected to act under the discreet direction of British officials. The most significant responsibility envisaged for the Protectorate Assembly in the immediate future was the election of twelve members to the Legislative Council.[57] The colonial government, under pressure to concede an elected majority in a body which the Colonial Office agreed could not be allowed to fall under Creole control,[58] clearly regarded this as a method of supplying black legislators who could (like the three nominated chiefs on the existing Council) be depended upon to vote under official direction.

Such transparent expedients were rejected not only by the Creoles but by educated leaders of Protectorate opinion, who now sought to combat the "conventional wisdom" that an unbridgeable gulf between the two sections of Sierra Leone would continue to preclude real progress towards self-government. The main lines of subsequent development are well known.[59] The Sierra Leone Organization Society, which held its first Annual General Meeting at Moyamba in June 1946, attracted support from a "growing body" of literate natives of the Protectorate[60] who were worried by government policy; in 1951 its alliance with some younger forward-looking Creoles and some chiefs brought into being the Sierra Leone Peoples' Party, which ten years later would become heir to the colonial government. This however was not because it had developed a mass organization capable of wresting the initiative from the British, but because the British time-table had been overthrown by the multiple crises of the post-war Commonwealth, and the consequent need to accept accelerated decolonization in the Gold Coast and Nigeria. Once more the assumptions which changed British West African policy over-rode the pessimistic expectations of local officials; if Sierra Leone fell too far out of step with new policies elsewhere in West Africa it would become a political embarrassment – and perhaps a financial liability. When elections were eventually held to a reconstituted Legislative Council in 1951, Governor Beresford-Stooke turned to the SLPP to co-operate in the first steps towards a transfer of power, not as the trained and designated successors of the Empire, but (given the intransigently particularist line of Bankole Bright and the Creole "old guard") as the only credible collaborators in sight.

THE FIRST DECOLONIZERS

Yet during the 1940s the need to prepare for decolonization had not been forgotten by all British officials in Sierra Leone, and some SLPP leaders at least had been coached for their new roles. Lord Caradon has spoken of the concern of members of the colonial service to ensure for their African subjects a "start in freedom"; though he may in his own generation have been more exceptional in this than memory suggests, such concern was certainly present among the post-war intake.[61] Still more was such a concern shared by some of the specialist professional workers brought to Africa to inaugurate new programmes under the Development and Welfare Acts. Educationists are perhaps the prime example; many who came to work in the new colleges (above all in their extra-mural departments) had a very clear commitment to the goal of preparation for self-government, and in the teaching of groups and individuals might be explicitly envisaging their future roles within, say, a parliamentary democracy of Socialist inclination. Social scientists whose visits to Africa were now sponsored by the Colonial Research Committee might also assist in the political education of those whom they saw as potential inheritors; in Sierra Leone, the correspondence of Dr Kenneth Little with his colleagues in the Fabian Colonial Bureau could provide illustration of this. But perhaps the most striking and most successful example of a new decolonizer was provided by Edgar Parry, a former official of the Municipal and General Workers Union, who in the early summer of 1942 arrived in Freetown as Assistant Labour Officer.

Colonial Office recognition of the need to pay special attention to labour problems has been reflected in the appointment of Major G. St. J. Orde-Browne as Labour Adviser in 1938, and of H. A. Nisbet as Labour Secretary in Sierra Leone in July 1939. Both men were former administrative officers. Their broad assumption was that labour policy was essentially a matter of enforcing minimum standards of welfare in such matters as diet, housing, and health; and also the enactment and enforcement of rudimentary legislation covering workmen's compensation and the machinery of industrial bargaining. Though the encouragement of trade unions along British lines was part of their responsibility – and Nisbet, anxious not to leave the initiative to the Youth League, did take this seriously – this was not a direction in which the pre-war Colonial Service was well prepared to lead.[62] With the entry of the Labour Party into the Coalition government, however, the Colonial Office was led to accept that the British trade union movement itself might have a specific contribution to make to the development of African societies and the preparation of new elites to lead them. Early in 1941 the Colonial Office revealed that it was considering a few "experimental appointments" of trade unionists to posts in selected colonies – hoping thus to offset "irresponsible and misguided leadership" and to "assist and encourage the adoption of collective bargaining in preference to the strike weapon". Freetown was somewhat reluctantly persuaded to adopt this approach, and this provided the opportunity for Parry's appointment.[63]

Dr H. E. Conway has noted Parry's success in promoting a system of industrial relations, based upon British experience, which gave Sierra Leone some twenty years of industrial harmony.[64] The emphasis of the Labour Department's work shifted from the wide-ranging responsibility for social welfare favoured by Orde-Browne towards encouraging the organization of trade unions, and providing them with opportunities for constructive achievement through Wages Boards and Joint Industrial Councils. This new attitude was exemplified as early as 1943, when the Colonial Office was surprised to find Parry evaluating the policies of the iron-mining Development Company (which administrators had repeatedly criticized for inadequate concern for workers' welfare, but which had now come round to encourage the formation of trade unions) more highly than those of the Selection Trust (which provided better housing and rations but exercised firm authoritarian control over their diamond concession).[65] By 1946 Parry, though still suffering "a considerable amount of social ostracism" from local officials,[66] enjoyed a high reputation in the Colonial Office, and succeeded to the senior post of Commissioner of Labour; in 1948 he returned to London as Assistant, and later Deputy, Labour Adviser to the Secretary of State.

Parry did not work to encourage trade unionism merely as a means of securing harmonious industrial relations, but as one important condition for the growth of social democracy in Africa. An enthusiastic correspondent of Rita Hinden and the Fabian Colonial Bureau, Parry's wider aims included promotion of Labour Parties in West Africa – a cause which in 1946 he attempted to urge on Dennis Healey in Transport House.[67] He fulminated against the ignorance and indifference of his European colleagues towards wider political issues, urging on his Fabian friends the need for "the application of a long-term policy".[68] As far as his immediate responsibilities were concerned this meant taking the initiative in trade union matters out of the hands of voluble demagogues like Wallace-Johnson – "the most objectionable and unscrupulous person I have met in political life"[69] – and encouraging labour leaders who could combine talents for honest and efficient organization with realistic visions of a democratic future for Sierra Leone.

Surveying the scene at the end of the war, Parry had been pessimistic about such a future. "The general impression held by many people at home of masses of colonial peoples stirring against colonial domination is certainly not true of this place," he wrote; while the Protectorate remained "contented in a bovine sort of way", Creole opposition to the Municipality Ordinance seemed "peevish" and "vituperative". But Parry saw promise among younger trade unionists, especially in a full-time official "of my own making".[70] Three months later Rita Hinden learned the name of Parry's "principal discovery": Siaka Stevens, a former worker for the Development Company, whom Parry had encouraged first to organize the labour force at Marampa and Pepel and had now moved to Freetown as General Secretary of the United Mineworkers Union. "He has a lot to learn but he knows it and shows an insatiable appetite for the knowledge he stands in need of," wrote Parry, suggesting that he might receive "sympathetic guidance and encouragement" through officials of the West African Council.[71] At a meeting in Nigeria Stevens had already been elected secretary of a West African Federation of Trade Unions (apparently a premature and abortive attempt to follow up the WFTU conference of 1945); early in 1946 he duly became first secretary of the Sierra Leone Trades Union Congress.[72]

A basic reason for the rise of Stevens and the consequent eclipse of Wallace-Johnson was the former's skill in obtaining benefits for his members through the industrial machinery which Parry had promoted. By 1946 the wages board system was working well; not only were the workers apparently well satisfied with the increases negotiated there, but the employers were anxious to buttress the system by deducting trade union dues from wages. "In fact they want to go as far towards the closed shop as they can. I had nothing to do with this. It's this man Stevens. He seems to have fascinated the mine owners."[73] In 1947 Joint Industrial Councils were established, with similar euphoria.[74] But Parry also saw Stevens and his colleagues as partners or collaborators in social-democratic decolonization; his immediate ambition was "a trade union and Labour movement . . . with its hooks well into both sides of Transport House and not tied up with some fake African nationalist party".[75]

Siaka Stevens' response to Parry's social democratic idealism was encouraging. In 1947–8, he visited Britain on a government scholarship, dividing his time between studies at Ruskin College and attachment to the head-quarters of the British TUC. During this period he established friendly relations with Rita Hinden and other leaders of the Fabians, corresponding regularly and fluently; an article he contributed to their journal, *Empire*, testifies to the "inestimable value" of "Labour Advisers . . . of the right type". It is true there were notes of increasing criticism of British policy; in particular he complained that officials were still using chiefs and other traditional authorities to dominate the new Councils in the Protectorate, ignoring "the general awakening among common men and women all over the world".[76] "As far as the repairing of the old Imperial edifice is concerned the Labour Government has done very well indeed," he wrote. "But what is needed is a totally new structure."[77] These criticisms became sharper after the Accra riots, and Stevens' own return to Sierra Leone in October 1948; how, he now asked, could Fabians reconcile "all this talk about free grants to the colonies from British taxpayers' money while at the same time we can see huge sums being taken out of the colonies in the form of profits"?[78] Yet this was frank talk among comrades, whose support was still desired and highly valued.

On the Wages Boards [Stevens wrote, in terms which might have surprised Parry], I used to be so full of anger against the bosses that I would feel like turning cannibal on them. I feel differently now. I realize now that the employers exploit us not because they are white men but because they are human beings, having in them all the frailties that man is heir to.[79]

When Siaka Stevens entered the Executive Council and assumed ministerial responsibility for Lands, Mines and Labour after the elections of 1951 he seemed to have been well prepared for the role of collaborator in a social-democratic programme of decolonization; and forward-looking Europeans placed high hopes upon such an able and robust collaborator. His future career would indeed by distinguished; but it was not to run smoothly along the lines envisaged by these decolonizers.

The evidence surveyed here does not suggest that, in Sierra Leone, there was any conscious plan to revert to a system of informal empire, or to transfer power to some neo-colonial collaborating elite. During the middle years of the war the Colonial Office began to urge local officials, usually against their judgement and inclination, to apply their "tentative plan for constitutional development"; but administrators showed little enthusiasm in preparing the bases for an autonomous state, and scepticism as to whether so small an African country could *ever* become fully independent long persisted. The dream of channelling political development through Native Authorities necessarily implied postponing self-government to so distant a date that planning was neither practical nor necessary; any alternative programme involved heavy dependence on Creoles, in administrative cadres and in politics, and they had been written off as possible inheritors of Empire.

Once official policy had become reluctantly committed to political change, those who took the commitment to self-government most seriously were indeed anxious to communicate democratic and Socialist values to their collaborators – just as in France the post-war years saw the apotheosis of the principled assimilationists. It might be said of both Empires that idealists with a vision of continuing Afro-European partnership now proved the most dedicated neo-colonialists. Given time they might have achieved a more thorough preparation; but in Sierra Leone as in much of French Africa the pace of change was set by external pressures, beyond their power to control. Although men like Parry may have laid some durable "cables" which will affect relationships, the societies which they have helped to create are by no means those which they intended.

4 Resisters, Collaborators, Heritors

AFTER-THOUGHTS ON "AFRICAN NATIONALISM"

The two preceding chapters, by concentrating on attempts by the British government to retain the political initiative in West Africa, have inclined towards a "decolonizing" interpretation of the end of colonial rule. They thus run contrary to a historiographical mainstream of the 1950s and 1960s, when the foundation of new states (and new universities) was celebrated by a great deal of historical writing about "African nationalism". This concept was eclectically used; Thomas Hodgkin's seminal study of 1956 presented a descriptive panorama embracing "any organization or group that explicitly asserts the rights, claims and aspirations of a given African society (from the level of the language-group to that of 'Pan-Africa') in opposition to European authority, whatever its institutional form and objectives".[1] But not all who adopted Hodgkin's approach shared his concern to analyse ideologies and social foundations of specific "nationalist" groups; the movements so comprehensively described were often equally comprehensively approved as powerful forces for progress towards indeterminate ends.

Much of this writing focused on the ideas and actions of educated leaders, who articulated their demands in language familiar to Western scholars. Even when it was recognized that their social background and experience had provided only limited contacts with the African masses, there was widespread hope that the bracing kiss of the "political kingdom" would awaken the sleeping beauties of new African nations. That indeed was the hope of the British decolonizers when they at last decided to seek the collaboration of an African middle class. And the political spokesmen of that class who set out to claim their inheritance were usually confident that they deserved the support of their countrymen.

Among their nationalist credentials, West African political leaders of the post-war period could point to records of resistance to colonial tyranny through the channels authorized by the colonial state – actions in the courts, articles in the press, protests in the Legislative Council. In the older generation Azikiwe could point to much spirited journalism and campaigning, and a spectacular acquittal on charges of seditious libel; though he did not know it, the British Colonial Secretary in 1943 had dubbed him "the biggest danger of the lot".[2] More spectacularly still, Nkrumah had been chief target for the sarcastic venom of the Watson Commission, the martyred "prison graduate" called from jail to form Ghana's embryonic national government. Clearly such men were authentically radical nationalists, who could claim to be liberators of their countries?

It would be patronizing and narrow-minded to question the authenticity of such acts of resistance, or to under-rate the courage which was needed to make them. But once again it must be emphasized that in West Africa "resistance" and "collaboration" were not polar opposites, but alternative responses to foreign rulers whose own behaviour was not uniformly oppressive. Constitutional opposition only made sense if there was a chance that the constitution might work in your favour. "Zik", having narrowly missed martyrdom at the hands of Sir Arnold Hodson's administration, could happily admire the Sunshine Governor's spirited adaptation of "The Teddy-Bear's Picnic", and cherish his generous wedding-present of Baldwin's speeches.[3] And Nkrumah, after the decisive victory of 1951, was prepared to co-operate with Arden-Clarke through what now seems the lengthy transitional period of six years. "*He* is being educated by *us*", one hopeful Fabian wrote in 1953;[4] exactly what Nkrumah learned is open to discussion, but he had clearly agreed to enroll in the class. Few if any contemporaries regarded this as dangerously compromising. Africans who had long urged the colonial masters to honour the contracts of partnership which their Victorian ancestors had promised could hardly refuse to respond when this seemed at last to be happening.

More broadly, it is now clear that the whole social stratum from which the nationalist leadership was drawn – whether called the middle class, the national bourgeoisie, the educated elite, or simply "the few",[5] had always been among the essential collaborators, and heirs-presumptive, of the colonial state. From humble, though often powerful, interpreters, clerks and court messengers right up the scale to learned barristers and Honourable Members of Legislative Council, they had essential roles to play. Even licensed critics like Azikiwe were part of the system; their occasional successful jousts with the government could actually help to legitimize its claims to liberal intentions. In the perspective of the 1970s the continuities between colonial and independent status may seem almost as striking as the innovations, and the "nationalism" professed by the founding fathers dwindles in importance. The term does not feature in the index of the authoritative *History of West Africa* edited by Professors Ajayi and Crowder, and in the text is chiefly used to describe the growth of "ethnic nationalism" among Asante and Igbo, Yoruba and Ewe.[6] The diverse "initiatives" or "responses" of specific groups of Africans are now seen as a more profitable focus for studying the "liberating" forces of the period than the ideologies of nationalist leaders.

It would be unfair and misleading to imply that the "bourgeois nationalists" did not desire or intend to serve the interests of the African masses; even in 1915, J. E. Casely Hayford had admired the success of Prophet Harris in reaching a mass audience still beyond the range of any merely secular prophet.[7] By 1941 Hailey perceived that political activists might now find more favourable conditions; he regarded "trouble arising from economic causes . . . questions connected with wages or the living conditions of industrial labour or the prices paid for commodities of native production" as likely sources of future trouble.[8] Africans like Wallace-Johnson, who had learned a little from the Communists, were already looking to the growing proletariat in ports, capitals and mining centres. Modern scholars likewise have found urban societies easier to penetrate than those of rural Africa. "In order to account for contemporary African nationalism", Hodgkin asserted in 1956, "one must study the new 'proto-industrial' towns" (p. 18). Although one of his chapters was entitled "Workers and Peasants", it proved to consist almost wholly of a discussion of trade unions, "partly for the practical reason that there is rather more material available; partly because of the intrinsic importance of trade unions in the history of almost every modern nationalism" (p. 117). And indeed African labourers had shown their capacity to take industrial action in defence of their interests as early as the nineteenth century.

The general thesis about the importance of an urban proletariat, taught by Marx and demonstrated by Lenin in 1917, had been apprehended by colonial governments too. Hence their appointment, during and after the war, of experienced trade unionsts like Edgar Parry, eager to encourage labour movements along "healthy" lines and to frustrate those who, like Wallace-Johnson, might mislead the masses. Hence too the interest taken by the rival federations of French trade unions, and the subsequent injection into Africa of the rifts which the Cold War produced among the unions of the "developed" world. African trade unionists came to resent such interference, and sought to build labour movements free from foreign direction; while doing so they often established close alliances with nationalist politicians which might involve accepting their leadership, and eventually their control. But despite the clarity and vigour with which they could defend their class interests, African workers were not numerous nor powerful enough to transform the political movements to which they adhered. At best they might provide them with leaders, like Sékou Touré or Siaka Stevens; more often (as in Ghana) they found their strength being harnessed to support the new political establishment, or the military regimes which superseded them.

So students of the transfer of power, like those of colonial rule, must face the problems of the countryside. For colonial governments the key to tranquillity was to enlist the collaboration of African intermediaries who enjoyed legitimate authority (or less hopefully, to legitimize the authority of pre-selected collaborators). Students of the colonial period are increasingly addressing themselves to the question of how, and how far, this was done. For nationalists who aspired to claim the allegiance of the peasants (or "bushmen", to render a somewhat pejorative Anglo-Norman word into current Afro-English usage) it was similarly necessary to find alternative intermediaries, or to take over those of the colonial masters. Without the co-operation of those masters, this was not an easy thing to do; nor is it an easy process to study. Those who write of "peasant societies" need to see how traditions and customs learned through elders and kinsmen interact with the pressures of the market in a particular time and place – to bring both anthropology and economics to bear upon the conditions of actual human beings, preferably with the aid of Tawney's famous boots. It will be a long time yet before the few localized studies which have seriously attempted this can be securely connected to historical generalizations.

THE TRIUMPH OF THE CPP AND ITS RURAL BASE

Broad observations about the colonial situation can be made easily enough. British rulers – faced, as African politicians would later be faced, by the need to secure collaboration from extensive populations about whom they knew rather little – usually worked through traditional authorities – "chiefs" of one sort or another who were prepared to operate a colonial system on mutually acceptable terms. Even in 1945 there were still places – pre-eminently Northern Nigeria – where such partnerships, formalized in the structures of "indirect rule", still seemed stable; but there were more cases of "traditional authorities" already being transformed or undermined by the penetration of an unstable commercial economy. In 1937–8 cocoa hold-ups in the Gold Coast and protests in Western Nigeria provided focus for mass action by chiefs and farmers in the major areas of rural capitalism; peripheral areas whose commercial role was confined to supplying labour or growing food sometimes showed signs of movement too. Perception of the need for a political framework which could contain such pressures explains the government's growing concern, articulated by Hailey in 1942, to modify their administrative structures – by establishing stronger indirect rule in areas like Sierra Leone and the Southern Gold Coast where laxer system of over-rule had been tolerated, and by introducing representatives of "commoners" into Native Authorities which were proving too authoritarian or conservative.

The reforming impulse became more urgent as plans for economic development multiplied, and notional time-scales for the transfer of power began to contract. It reached a climax in Creech Jones's circular despatch of 25 February 1947, urging the need for "the development of an efficient, democratic system of local government".[9] Those institutional changes which followed were complemented by the encouragement of "voluntary associations" which might channel the energies which were being politically awakened – community development schemes, officially-sponsored co-operatives, even potential centres of radicalism like the People's Educational Association on the Gold Coast, were all involved in "the slow work of nation building".[10] As the character of central government was modified, attempts were thus made to legitimize new policies with the "new men" of rural society, but without antagonizing old chiefly elites.

During this transitional period, "nationalist" politicians needed to enter the competition for mass rural support for the first time. Although few of them showed great interest in undertaking the practical work of local government for the sake of direct results, they were inevitably drawn in when local councils were designated as electoral colleges for the new central legislature. British policy-makers had calculated that bodies of local worthies, elected by shrewd peasants who knew them well, would not easily be penetrated by facile demagogues, and often this proved correct. The crucial contrary case (which expedited the abandonment of this expedient of indirect elections) was of course the unforeseen success of Nkrumah's Convention Peoples' Party in the Gold Coast election of February 1951. As a perceptive observer later pointed out, the administration had virtually created a structure around which the party could build its organization. The problems of registering the new electorate in Southern Gold Coast and Asante produced "a tacit alliance . . . between the CPP members and the colonial officials", without which even the modest success rate of 40 per cent could not have been achieved. Working through such "voluntary" associations as improvement societies, young men's organizations and above all farmers' associations, the CPP proceeded to secure 1950 out of 2713 votes in the electoral colleges and to return its candidates in 29 of the 33 rural seats.[11]

In general terms, the conditions which permitted these urban-based politicians to penetrate rural society are clear enough: Akan political traditions which allowed commoners or "young men", organized in *asafo* companies, not only to de-stool chiefs, but to organize opposition to colonial policies,[12] and the long-standing grievances of the country's 200 000 cocoa-farmers,* recently aggravated by maladroit measures to enforce the "cutting-out" of trees affected by swollen shoot. It was crucially important for the CPP to

---

* The Census Commissioner of 1948 estimated that approximately 214 420 persons, (including 64 400 women) out of a total population of 4 118 450, were "engaged in growing cocoa" (not including unskilled workers engaged in carrying beans); and 1367 males were "engaged in marketing cocoa"; 180 105 persons described themselves as owners, part owners or tenants of cocoa-farms, most but not all being farmers as well; hence the Commissioner concluded that wage-labourers did not exceed 40 000. These figures indicated that 13 per cent of the male population of the Colony, 21.5 per cent in Asante and 8.1 per cent in Togoland, were engaged in cocoa cultivation. *The Gold Coast. Census of Population, 1948* (London and Accra, 1950), pp. 20–4.

secure the support of farmers' leaders – men like Ashie Nikoi who had already established their credentials in the thirty-year-old struggle to establish greater control over the marketing and export of cocoa. In December 1949 Nikoi and John Ayew founded the Ghana Farmers' Congress in association with the CPP; and in Austin's words, "once the farmers accepted a nationalist party as the political expression of their own grievances it spread through the southern rural areas like fire through a dry wood."[13] Without such mobilisation of rural support the CPP's electoral coup of 1951 would have been impossible.

It is still unclear exactly how this success was achieved within particular localities; students of political sociology might wish to know what *types* of "cocoa-farmer" (share-croppers, immigrant farmers, or citizen landholders) were most likely to act politically, and under what circumstances. In Agona, immigrant farmers did not regard themselves as entitled to register for the elections; but in Akim Abuakwa, Ashie Nikoi seems to have drawn heavily on immigrant support in his (narrowly unsuccessful) campaign against the influence of the Ofori Atta family. But Akim Abuakwa was an exceptional place, and in many districts there had still been little opportunity for political cleavages to develop. More typical may have been the case of Ahafo, where the electoral college, composed of farmers and leaders of local improvement societies who had been recruited into the CPP, was largely returned unopposed.[14]

For present purposes, such problems are of secondary importance. The essential point is that in 1951 urban-based "nationalists" obtained mass support in rural areas by promising that when they inherited the resources of the colonial state (including the surpluses currently being accumulated by the Cocoa Marketing Board), rural commoners would benefit. The victorious CPP did not wholly forget this, and farmers did receive some return from the world cocoa boom; yet the general tendency of the new regime was to continue the colonial practice of extracting funds from the rural areas to be applied in accordance with the "national interest", as interpreted from the capital of a bureaucratic state. And a substantial slice of the cocoa revenue was now appropriated for the benefit of the CPP machine, if not of individual party militants. Colonial machinery was taken over, not destroyed; party agents joined the chiefs and the Africanized administration in the government of rural Ghana.

POLITICIANS, CHIEFS AND PEASANTS: VARIATIONS ON A THEME

The lengthened historical perspective of the 1970s suggests that this Ghanaian experience provided a sort of outline scenario which other countries would follow. During the 1950s a succession of political parties with essentially urban bases became collaborators in the transfer of political power. Some achieved this role by demonstrating popular support, others had it thrust upon them by governments committed to policies of accelerated decolonization. As they moved into the offices of their colonial masters, the nationalists also inherited the problem of legitimizing the authority of capital cities over dispersed rural populations; sometimes they inherited colonial solutions as well, sometimes they created alternative structures, and alternative problems, of their own. There is one striking exception to such generalizations: Guiné-Bissao, where the old rural hierarchies on whom the Portuguese had relied would probably have proved too weak to become credible heritors even if colonial policy had recognized them as such. Here a genuinely revolutionary movement, created through a conscious effort to identify the needs and problems of the "bushmen" in the villages, can convincingly claim to have liberated not only its own country, but that of its former rulers.[15] But elsewhere, one group or another of African politicians found themselves operating machinery devised by the colonial power for administering the rural areas on which colonial economies largely rested.

The most illuminating account of what political activity actually meant during this period is provided by a richly detailed biography of Adegoke Adelabu, an ebullient Yoruba who before a fatal road accident in 1958 had achieved genuine mass support in and around the city of Ibadan. The early career of this ambitious and restless man had little to do with anything which might be called "nationalism"; frustrated by the limited recognition afforded to his talents in colonial Nigeria, he saw his opportunities in this sprawling pre-colonial city, whose government the British hoped to modernize through educated commoners of a more sober type. Adelabu's insights into complex local issues of status, kinship and economic interest, and his picturesque rhetoric and invective (to which he soon learned to give an anti-colonial slant when appropriate), proved invaluable assets during the age of decolonization. In 1951, when the process of constitutional reform obliged aspirant nationalist leaders to seek local support, Adelabu's populistic Ibadan Tax-Payers' Association, or *Mabolaje*, decided to support Azikiwe's National Council of Nigeria and the Cameroons, and Adelabu himself enjoyed a speedy though temporary rise to ministerial office in Lagos.

Adelabu's spirited belabouring of local issues gave him genuine popularity among the *mekunnu*, or common people; but it would be misleading to imagine mass involvement even in the local politics of Ibadan District. The *Mabolaje*'s electoral successes were based on low registration, small turn-outs, and uncontested victories in rural constituencies. Like the CPP they spoke of rural development, and voiced the opposition of cocoa-farmers to compulsory "cutting-out", but their main preoccupation was with issues affecting access to status or wealth within the city. Adelabu argued that: "The rural people have no experience of local Government operations. Their best training-ground will be for their first elected representative to sit along with more experienced city representatives in a comprehensive assembly."[16] Ibadan provided no exception to the general concentration by those elected to office during the 1950s on improving the amenities of the towns, and the emoluments of politicians and government servants who lived there, at the expense of rural tax-payers. The farmers, as they later told a foreign scholar, believed themselves "too poor" to take political initiatives – at least until 1969, when the violent protests known as *Agbekoya* ("the farmers renounce suffering") forcefully recalled unfulfilled promises of earlier years.[17]

This pattern of urban dominance was modified slightly where rural hierarchies seemed strong enough to take the strains of transfer. Northern Nigeria of course provides the classical case of this: the Northern Peoples' Congress, favoured partner of the British until 1966, was created for this role by aristocrats descended from the ruling elites of the Sokoto and Borno empires. In Sierra Leone there was continuity of collaboration for very different reasons. The Sierra Leone Peoples' Party, as suggested above, became the heir of the colonial government largely for lack of alternatives.[18] Originating in the earnest desire of certain urban-based Africans to reconcile the peoples of Colony and Protectorate, it had by the 1951 election neither converted the Creoles nor established a base in the Protectorate independent of the chiefs, among whom only Julius Gulama of Kaiyamba could be counted an active supporter. None of the eight chiefs whom the District Councils elected to the central legislature was primarily a party man; they agreed to support Dr Milton Margai partly in reaction against the opposition's Creole particularism, partly in anticipation of favours to come. They did not seem promising agents of popular mobilization.

Despite the hopes of British administrators, the reform of native administration begun in 1937 had still not achieved spectacular results; the accelerated political time-table was running far ahead of the basic work of "nation-building". Development brought new opportunities for chiefs to extract resources from their subjects, which were not matched by effective constitutional controls; the newly-established District Councils, which chiefs dominated, provided new methods of raising revenue which paternalistic District Commissioners could not control. Indeed, at least one District Council President declared himself to have become "the Black DC."[19] The priorities of these chiefs were not those of the British officials who had conceived the development policy; many of them, observing that certain commoners were benefiting from the increased patronage of the colonial government, or from the early stages of the diamond rush, felt that it was the duty of the peasantry to improve the status of their "natural rulers" (which it was true had never been very glorious). The intermediary was surely worthy of his hire; as a former trader and store-keeper who became chief at Makeni told his subjects, "now that I am chief I have nowhere to eat from except you".[20] In November 1955 Alikali Modu III, Paramount Chief of Port Loko since 1949 and Legislative Councillor since 1951, demanded as a *second* contribution to the construction of a modern house, a levy of 5s per tax-payer; together with an increase of 7s 6d approved by the District Council, this raised the liability of the Port Loko tax payer from £1 5s 0d to £1 17s 6d per head.[21] By later standards this may not sound an intolerable imposition; but it triggered a widespread rising through the southern part of the Northern Province.

Subsequent enquiries revealed much about those on whose collaboration the British and the SLPP leaders were relying for the transfer of power in Sierra Leone. Unauthorized fines, exactions and levies, demands for unpaid labour for the personal profit of the chief, arbitrary punishments and contemptuous behaviour – acts of petty tyranny which colonial rule had failed to control – seemed actually to be increasing under the new regime. Widespread resentment was focused on the increases in taxation, and voiced by articulate local leaders like Peter Kamara, who seems to have become something of a popular hero among the Temne around Port Loko. Spokesmen who had heard of the violent demonstration in Freetown the previous February[22] declared themselves to be "strikers", and complained that "power had now passed into the hands of their own people, who were not fit to govern them".[23]

It seemed as though the "bushmen" were about to seize the political initiative from the chiefs; but this did not happen. The "disturbances" were followed by some changes of personnel, but not of system. Although the Northern province later became the base from which the All Peoples' Congress mounted its opposition to an increasingly divided and discredited SLPP, the extent to which it built on the populism which the strikers expressed, rather than on rival contenders for chiefly office, is hard to judge. Peter Kamara died in his village a few years after the rising; and the other village Hampdens named in the Cox Report are not, immediately at least, identifiable as future APC militants. Chiefs censured by the Commissioners were removed from office – including two SLPP leaders, Alikali Modu III and the Honourable Minister without Portfolio, Bai Farima Tass II; but it is not clear that their subjects found life radically changed under their successors. At Port Loko unpaid labour is now offered for impressive "self-help" schemes sponsored not by the chief but by the APC – which, besides a much-needed hospital extension, a mosque, and the Bai Bureh Memorial Hall, have erected a luxurious Presidential Lodge. Meanwhile the former Alikali Modu III, having prospered in business, has publicly announced his adhesion to the new regime.

In French-ruled Africa, as in Portuguese Guinea, the option of an alliance with chiefs was unattractive to urban nationalists. French administrators (subject to more temporary or localized variations than is often recognized) had worked to weaken traditional authorities, and incorporate "chiefs" into their own centralized bureaucracy; like the *intendants* of the *ancien regime*, their successes prepared the ground for revolutionary reconstructions to follow. In the words of a shrewd French observer, "the colonial situation, while founded upon essentially inegalitarian principles as regards relations between colonizers and colonized, carried within itself seeds which proved to be democratic in regard to relations between the different social groups of the colonized".[24] But like the men of 1789, the spokesmen of African nations find it difficult to realize the new order which they promised in forms which matched the needs and aspirations of the peasants.

Some certainly tried. In Guinea the authority of the chiefs (which before colonial rule was broadly equivalent to that of their kinsmen in Sierra Leone) was already effectively discredited by 1957, when the urban radicals of the *Parti Démocratique de Guinée* acted with disillusioned French administrators to suppress the institution.[25] Hence, when Sékou Touré decided to reject the terms which de Gaulle offered next year for his new Community, the French had no intermediaries capable of resisting the PDG cadres, who successfully polled 95 per cent of the votes in the referendum. The victorious party now set out to unite the peoples of this sprawling country's four regions into a revolutionary nation. What went wrong with this admirable design – and how seriously – has been the subject of many spirited political analyses which cannot be reviewed here, but which seem to agree, at least, that the elaborate new party bureaucracy is far from universally popular, or successful in promoting its professed egalitarian goals.

In the French Trust Territory of Cameroun, an African attempt to break with colonial patterns of collaboration failed for very different reasons. The *Union des Populations du Cameroun*, whose "radical nationalism" was originally fostered among enterprising Bamileke farmers facing competition from privileged French *colons*, and among Bassa who were becoming proletarianized by the capital-intensive development of Sanaga-Maritime, was by 1955 beginning to consolidate its support in well-organized branches throughout the country. The end of the cocoa-boom provided conditions in which radical nationalists could expect more broadly-based support. This was precisely what the French authorities feared; they responded by military repression (leading to the only prolonged colonial war of the decolonization period in France's tropical colonies), but also by building up a coalition of alternative collaborators to whom power could be safely transferred. Although the UPC remained strong in the rural areas most strongly affected by the colonial economy, traditional elites elsewhere (especially in the Centre and North) could still be enlisted to support the more conservative form of independence conceded by the French in 1960. This went much further than originally intended, and the UPC could claim to have hastened the change of course in French African policy after 1956: but hardly in the hoped-for direction of revolutionary renewal.[26]

In 1978 the most durable of the successor states in French-speaking Black Africa seem to be those which did secure collaboration from established rural hierarchies. President Senghor owes much of his dominant position in Senegal to his early concern to enlist rural support in a colony traditionally dominated by the sophisticated urban politics of the *quatre communes*; yet the powerful political machine he created was not "designed for any purpose so imprudent as mass 'mobilization', but [effectively incorporated] enough of existing rural leadership (*marabouts*, tribal aristocrats, traders) to make political life difficult or . . . virtually impossible for organized opposition".[27] The "African socialism" associated with the new regime has left most Senegalese peasants untouched. A scholar who has identified herself closely with the life of a village near Bakel has written movingly of the cycle of poverty which continues to drive a massive migration overseas, and of the irrelevance to locally perceived problems of the technocratic development schemes which are sponsored through Dakar.[28] Despite the Senegalese talent for cultural and institutional *métissage* of which the President often boasts, the continuities of Senegalese life are on the whole more impressive than the innovations.

At the end of the Second World War it did seem that politics in the Ivory Coast might take a more turbulent course. As in Cameroun, a sizeable population of *colons* enjoyed much influence with the administration, especially on the sensitive matter of access to supplies of forced labour. On this issue the prosperous African farmers of the *Syndicat Agricole Africain*, which provided the nucleus of Houphouët-Boigny's Ivoirien branch of the RDA, secured a good deal of broad popular support, and their success was demonstrated in the Constituent Assembly election of 1946. To resist the pressure which the *colons* could still exercise in Paris Houphouët-Boigny relied on the alliance of French Communists; as the Cold War intensified this drew increased hostility from French administrators also. By 1949 Houphouët-Boigny, like his neighbour Nkrumah, seemed to have become committed to a violently anti-colonial confrontation. But during 1950-1 the French premier Pleven and his colonial minister Mitterand (representing two generations of "colonial reformers") moved to avert the perils of another colonial war by "institutionalizing the RDA" through programmes of constructive reform and increased economic assistance within the French Union. Houphouët-Boigny and his associates, seeing more tangible prospects in such collaboration than in continued resistance, therefore agreed to a change of course comparable in importance to that which Nkrumah was making in Accra. Internally, this involved increasingly reliance upon African entrepreneurs, professional men and substantial farmers (many connected with traditional chiefs) who stood to gain from the growing flows of French investment and aid, rather than on the rural masses whom they had begun to mobilize. Even had the local RDA leaders wished to promote revolutionary changes in rural society, the new course of Ivoirien nationalism now made this impossible.

INTERIM EVALUATIONS

During the 1950s, many who wrote enthusiastically about the triumph of "African nationalism" were excited by the creative possibilities of the period. Europeans with varied political convictions welcomed the spectacle of resisters turning into collaborators in expectation of harmonious benefits all round. A generation sceptical about imperial missions welcomed the transfer into African hands of the thankless responsibility of administering the African farmers who produced their cocoa and groundnuts; only a few paternalistic administrators feared that the extraction of these resources from the countryside might henceforth proceed with less restraint. Politicians concerned about the international position of Britain and France were reassured by Nkrumah's zeal to become involved in Commonwealth diplomacy, and by Houphouët—Boigny's position as anchorman in the last governments of the Fourth, and the first of the Fifth Republic. International business seemed ready enough to adjust to the new political conditions (and to opportunities provided by new aid programmes) in expectation of continued commercial expansion along broadly established lines. Intellectuals sympathetic to African liberation shared in the general euphoria. Their doyen, Thomas Hodgkin, ended his book of 1956 trusting that rational decolonization "need not mean the breaking or weakening of trade or cultural connections between Europe and Africa, or a lessening of African interest in securing co-operation of European specialists. It might well in fact stimulate this kind of interchange" (p. 190).

European expectations in the later 1970s are less euphoric. Economic indicators vary greatly. Oil revenues have enabled

Nigerians to plan developments, and to make miscalculations, on the grand scale; in the Ivory Coast African enterprises of many sorts are growing, though largely in the wake created by the much increased involvement of French capital. But elsewhere the talk may be of "growth without development" on the periphery of the international economy; in some countries, even production of the old export crops or mineral staples has declined, reflecting deteriorating terms of external trade, internal disequilibrium, or depletion of natural resources. As far as the specific interests of the former metropolis are concerned, French economic influence in her former territories has generally been maintained rather better than that of Britain, whose relations with West Africa, as with India, show clear signs of what Michael Lipton has called "post-colonial inertia".

Hopes for vital and authentically African political life have receded even further. Ideals cherished in opposition rarely help those who have inherited the colonial state to redress inequalities which are built into its very foundations. Some yield to the temptations of money and power, others to the more invidious and respectable temptation not to rock the boat while it remains seaworthy. Attempts to change colonial structures meet resistance from honourable men (Africans as well as Europeans, *fonctionnaires* and academics as well as capitalists) with interests in preserving them; and there are always respectable colonial precedents for repressing those who threaten the delicate fabric of public order. Basil Davidson, that staunch friend of African freedom, now sees "African nationalism" in melancholy perspective, as an attempt by an over-confident "few" to recreate the nation-state of capitalist Europe within colonial enclosures which have proved ill prepared for its structures. While recognizing the virtues and the courage of particular nationalists, Davidson clearly regards most of the new political establishments as fatally alienated from what he calls the historic "charters" of African peoples; only the PAIGC, in his view, has through armed struggle recovered the potentiality to build a truly African nation.[29] Few indeed would claim that the "political kingdom" has yet brought either the economic revolution preached by prophets of capitalist enterprise, or the new social order which idealists saw lying just beyond the end of empire.

Possibly this prevailing reaction towards one form or another of historical pessimism has gone too far. Clearly both nationalists and decolonizers made grave miscalculations, and fatal oversimplifications; but not everything in West Africa has changed for the worse. It is hard to avoid recognizing tragic failings among the first generation of national governments (often under stresses and temptations of which few of their critics can have the slightest experience). But the administrative and judicial cadres which the decolonizers finally decided to sponsor have lasted much better, and sometimes shown greater understanding of the needs of the new states. Military men trained in similar traditions have often proved capable of exercising wider political responsibilities, though with varying results. (Whether they have laid a better structural foundation than the British for the unity of the peoples of Nigeria, is at the time of writing crucially in doubt.)

It likewise seems necessary to avoid premature judgements on the intellectual elites which centre on the new universities which have proliferated so greatly since the days of Elliot. It is always easy to accuse academics of "irrelevance", of enjoying comfortable incomes in return for performing flaccid variations on meaningless themes; but there is a solid record of achievements, political as well as intellectual. (Probably a study of the many Nigerian academics who have become Commissioners under the military government would show a capacity for innovation well above the average.) Their British colleagues often fail to appraise these achievements with detachment; conscious of African failures to meet great challenges they may forget their own failings as part of the academic community which has nurtured and deeply influenced this intellectual elite. Academic, political and personal reactions become intertwined in ways which it is difficult and uncomfortable to appraise objectively.

Failing some unattainable Olympian detachment, frankly subjective approaches seem preferable to suppression. Some of these follow in the second part of this book.

Part II
Some Professorial Footnotes

5 Changing Views from an Ivory Tower

Those whose studies seek to discern deep currents of historical change are often surprised by the role which chance has played in their own lives. I became a student of history because a prolonged teenage illness induced an interest in the political news-reporting of 1938 and because this interest was then seized and developed by a gifted teacher of European history, Leslie Gilbert. I became interested in the non-European world because miscellaneous military duties in Malaya during 1946 introduced me to a society of whose rich historical background my courses in wartime Manchester had said little. I began to think specifically (and ignorantly) about Africa because, on returning to study European diplomacy in Manchester, I was privileged to enjoy the friendship of a remarkable Nigerian fellow-student, Eni Njoku. By 1952 I had married a wife who was also anxious to work overseas for a time: a job in Malaya might still have been tempting, but Fourah Bay College advertised first; and my intellectual course was set for a quarter-century.

Sheila and I knew, of course, that the job had political implications, in the broadest sense. As Labour Party members with Christian beliefs and Fabian tendencies we believed strongly that Africans had the right to govern themselves, but that they would only be enabled to do so after a period of intensive preparatory "nation-building", during which the architects as well as the master-craftsmen must be foreign. I suppose we shared the cosy but not wholly unserviceable ambiguity of most European social-democrats, later expressed by a Labour politician whom I heard declare that the right of Africans to determine their own destinies was unconditional, but that it was essential to provide them with Socialist economies first. In other words, our optimism was largely typical of that phase of decolonization whose historical characteristics are discussed in the first section of this volume.

The grand design of the nation-builders had been based on the "British model" of parliamentary democracy; in the Gold Coast the Coussey Committee had solemnly declared this to be fully compatible with African political traditions, on the authority of a young British scholar commissioned by Nuffield College to study Legislative Councils through the printed sources available in England.[1] A necessary corollary of this was that, in the words of a recent British White Paper, "a lot of help was given to the development of education . . . with the motive, stated or not, of producing a corps of civil servants and other leaders in society who would be able to take over from expatriates".[2] The new University Colleges, and the Colleges of Arts, Science and Technology (for Fourah Bay had temporarily been relegated, protesting, into this second division of the Colonial Office's higher education league), eagerly accepted this role of training "counsellors" for these new democracies, as well as providing new "channels through which British ideas can flow into Africa".[3] In retrospect it may be thought that the whole enterprise was permeated by the terrible sin of paternalism; and certainly British academics involved did tend to express a deep sense of responsible concern, such as only parents can show, that these young institutions should develop healthily along lines which we had come to approve through our own experience.

Fourah Bay, though no longer young, felt in 1952 that its growth had been retarded. The conventional wisdom of Colonial Office planners was that a University College in Sierra Leone could not in the foreseeable future be financed, staffed, or supplied with qualified students; the country should therefore be content with a Regional College, exporting its university candidates to Ibadan or Accra. As an interim measure this former missionary college had been allowed to retain a University *Department*. In 1953–4 this had 119 students (exactly one-third of the College total), but more than half of these were Nigerians, and only 49 from Sierra Leone. There was a provisional air about many of its facilities, even as it became clear that the provisional was going to last; in 1950 the sum of £200 had been allocated to supplement the collection of theological treatises and outdated textbooks known as the Library, though by 1953 staff protests had secured an increase to £1250.[4] ("Why do these lecturers need more books?" one European member of Council allegedly demanded. "They can't have read everything in the Library already!") Indeed, the lecturers did take every opportunity to press for the full implementation of the idea of a colonial university, demanding not only books but such luxuries as honours courses and research programmes. African colleagues were particularly insistent that the status of the College should be clarified by physical separation of the non-graduating courses; those who believed a comprehensive college to be temporarily acceptable were regarded as dangerous compromisers, even though we seem to have anticipated one of the progressive causes of the 1970s.

But what united the academic battalions of the "second colonial invasion" with their African colleagues was more important than such tactical disagreements. We were all paternalistic enough to believe that our students would (as indeed they mostly did) become leaders in politics, administration, education and the professions, and that a British-style academic training in the liberal arts would be an excellent preparation for this. So we encouraged them to stretch their intellects to the limit on academic problems not of directly "developmental" importance; we insisted on defining "standards" according to externally-determined criteria. And if we had acted differently we would have been denounced by a vocal, though doubtless limited, African opinion whose imagination had been caught by Aggrey's slogan, "Nothing but the best is good enough for Africa". "Standards" had to be maintained even at the risk of cramping attempts to adapt curricula to the African environment. Although it seemed self-evident that my students ought to be addressing problems of African history, in 1952 there seemed to be insufficient published literature available to justify devoting a whole course to that subject and I lacked the knowledge and confidence to design one in any case; but it did seem feasible to vary the exclusive diet of British and European history by a course called "The Policies of the Great Powers in Africa". The College showed great concern that this might be regarded as a local soft option, and were only reassured when the University of Durham promised full parity of esteem in its Calendar entry.

Many of us also accepted enthusiastically our assigned role in civic education. In part, this took place in class, where there was a higher political content in my teaching of British history, probably also in that of Arthur Porter and Willie Conton, than would now seem appropriate. Socialist though I claimed to be, I tried to pass on some of the sceptical wisdom about the perils of consitutional rigidity and the merits of compromise which I had learned from Lewis Namier; my old teacher would have been considerably startled to hear himself cited in 1978 in President Stevens' address inaugurating one-party rule. Outside the classroom there was continuous political discussion with colleagues and students, who tended not so much to question whether parliamentary democracy was an appropriate goal as to suggest they were being taught an anglocentric version, and wished to learn more of the constitutional experience of France and the USA.

Another channel of political education was the Extra-Mural Department, which Walter Taylor had been seconded from Durham to establish in 1951. When he left I acted as *interimaire* for some months until the return of Edward Blyden III, grandson of a great pioneer in this field. The elder Blyden had in his time given Freetown a tradition of public lectures followed by discussion which it seemed not too hard to reconcile with familiar British patterns of university tutorial classes; after only a few weeks I found myself drafted into an inevitably naive attempt to relate Western political experience to that continuous process of constitution-making which provided the framework for decolonization during the 1950s. I might re-read my lectures with less embarrassment had my audience not included members of the Legislative and Executive Councils, who might be thought to require political education at a quite different level.

Although it was not difficult to find, and apparently satisfy, audiences for more or less formal classes conducted in the English language, the Department was anxious to reach less sophisticated audiences in the Protectorate, where settlement was dispersed, communications poor, and literacy probably well under 5 per cent. We were very conscious of the work being done in the Gold Coast by the talented team whose appointment had been inspired by Thomas Hodgkin. Walter Taylor had hoped to appoint Resident Tutors in each Province, and at his 1953 Easter School Sierra Leone established its own Peoples' Educational Association. Its aim was to "stimulate an informed public opinion" throughout the country, concentrating on such subjects as the new local government structures and increasingly developing work in African languages. But, apart from the government's noted Community Development scheme at Pujehun, informal education received little financial priority, and in any case there were few people with training or experience in this field. So our apparent successes were mostly with anglophone classes of anglophiles, anxious to participate in the new political structures. More time, more resources, and much more skill would have been needed for the wider enterprise.

As every parent knows, paternalism can be exhausting work. Besides academic and extra-mural duties, there were many jobs to be done in Freetown: reviving *Sierra Leone Studies*, consolidating Christopher Fyfe's marvellous salvage work on the National Archives . . . . After two years we felt ready for a steadier work-rhythm and a more conventional family life; the decision to leave was made easier since an African colleague was ready to take over. And indeed during the mid-fifties a change began to take place in Afro-British academic relationships. As the African Colleges became more firmly set on course, British universities began to advance from paternalism towards an attitude better described as avuncularism.

The characteristic of uncles is that, while they often have good advice and gifts to offer, they hold no formal responsibilities; conscious of their seniority and experience, genuinely anxious to be helpful, they may find tnis a comfortable role to play. For nephews, it is advantageous to have a selection of uncles, offering alternative sources of advice and assistance. After 1960, as foreign governments, international agencies and foundations became conscious that Africa was beginning to play more important roles in the affairs of the world, African universities entered on a period of euphoric expansion. The cautious assumptions of wartime planners about available finance, staff and students seemed ludicrously outdated as offers of new buildings, grants, endowments and scholarships showered in from often surprising directions. Many were misdirected, and others provided on terms which lay onerous burdens on the African tax-payer who would eventually have to take over the new projects; Sierra Leone is still suffering from American generosity in initiating an alternative channel of higher education at Njala. But it was a decade of extraordinary achievements, when African universities and African scholars asserted their presence in the world of learning at least as effectively as their governments were doing in the United Nations.

The sixties were a good time for uncles too. Once European academics accepted that African universities, like African governments, were for good or ill going to take their own decisions, the release from responsibility could have liberating effects. The process of devising schemes of constructive collaboration within well-financed "special relationships" brought opportunities for interesting travel and exhilarating discussions, often culminating in the avuncular satisfaction of contemplating new departments, well-trained graduates, exciting publications. And for those whose research interests were in African studies, there were additional bonuses.

The effects on the British academic world of this developing involvement with Africa are still difficult to assess. The visible evidence is striking. Centres of African Studies were established in Birmingham and Edinburgh, London and Sussex, Cambridge and York; scholars with African experience and/or research interests were appointed to posts in, and headships of, Departments whose interests had previously been bounded by the North Atlantic world; from 1963 the African Studies Association (UK) – and many smaller bodies, like the African Studies Group we established on a shoestring in Aberdeen – did their best to encourage that interpenetration of disciplinary approaches which had long characterized the best Africanist research. The effects of this academic activity on British opinion and policy towards contemporary problems, though less than they might have been, were not insignificant; the influence of those with Nigerian experience may have helped to prevent the disaster of a British recognition of the Biafran secession. But for British universities the greatest intellectual benefits may have come through the increased exposure of scholars, in varied branches of the social and natural sciences and of the humanities, to problems, hypotheses and concepts derived through the study of African data. In Chapter 7, I try to suggest what this may have meant for the development of historical studies.

African scholars may come to view this period of avuncularism rather differently. Immediately, the belated growth of British academic interest was helpful as well as gratifying; besides the offers of practical assistance and co-operation which it stimulated, the growth of African Studies in universities of established international standing helped to disperse any remaining local prejudices against the adaptation and Africanization of syllabuses. But when the new courses in African history were approved *because* they were taught in the University of London, what was this but academic neo-colonialism, however constructive? Even the importation of external examiners – a device enthusiastically accepted by African academics, which continues to provide many of us with opportunities for invigorating though strenuous travel – has had equivocal effects. Occasions for close professional discussion among fellow-workers are always welcome, and it is certainly important that those who are pursuing comparable objectives in different environments should be guided by the same principles and standards. But if standards are rigidly defined in relation to the academic conventions of a different society they can have cramping effects; there are departments in Africa whose regulations seem to make it harder for undergraduates to get a good (as distinct from a passable) degree than it would be in the UK. The development of medical education, where the academic conservatism has been powerfully reinforced by a prestigious profession with interests in high technology treatment, provides good examples of how avuncular advice can inhibit adaptation, even after the general acceptance that greater emphasis on community medicine would be appropriate to African needs.

It might have been expected that in African Studies the flow of advice would have been reversed, and that British universities would have benefited from the experience of colleagues engaged in developing new fields of study in Africa. But so far as formalized relations are concerned, this happened rarely: nobody became interested in financing regular journeys by external examiners from African to British universities. Perhaps this was because African Studies necessarily played a different role in African universities and one which is still in process of definition. The Institutes of African Studies set up during the sixties were often able to identify and sponsor urgent research tasks for archaeologists and ethnographers, students of languages and oral traditions; in rapidly changing societies these might be virtually rescue operations. But it proved more difficult to implement grand designs of introducing African students to the multi-disciplinary study of the environment, societies and cultures of their own continent; specialized institutes do not always provide the best framework for the integration of knowledge. And it seems that it may actually be easier to provide clear (though consequently superficial) perspectives on distant continents. An African university which established a Centre of European Studies might find that it achieved a sharper focus than some which exist in Europe – and it might contribute usefully to Africans' perceptions of their position in the world.

For in the later 1970s the importance for Africans of their relations with foreign powers is perhaps clearer than it was in the confident morning of independence. Political euphoria about the transfer of parliamentary democracy and the future of Afro-European relations began to evaporate during the early sixties, largely as a result of successive Congo crises; but the climate deteriorated rapidly after the unilateral declaration of Rhodesian independence in November 1965, which many African interpreted as the beginning of a colonial counter-offensive.[5] Europeans in turn grew disenchanted by the succession states they had helped to launch. By 1967 parliamentary institutions had been destroyed, temporarily at least, in each West African Commonwealth state except The Gambia, and a tragic civil war was putting Nigeria's very survival in jeopardy. The dictatorship which Idi Amin established in Uganda after 1971 became simply the crowning symbol of the shipwreck of Fabian optimism.

African universities, like armies and public services, proved more durable, and their international relations were not immediately affected too drastically by political upheavals. Indeed, disenchantment with existing regimes may actually have encouraged some foreign donors to invest in the education of the next generation of leaders. Thanks largely to resources, energy and optimism supplied from North America, the number of universities and the range of their activities grew far more rapidly than British planners once thought conceivable; and their senior posts were increasingly filled by Africans who felt justly proud of their achievement and confident in their collective capacities. By 1970, when I spent a year teaching in the University of Ibadan, it was clear that the age of avuncularism was merging into a period of cousinhood, during which self-confident African institutions would deal with foreign members of the academic extended family as equals, deciding which to cultivate, and which to leave alone.

But relations between cousins are perhaps more often correct than cordial. The mid-seventies have seen a distinct cooling of interest in Africa among British academics, whose own period of euphoric expansion has ended sharply. Many share the prevalent national mood of introspection; others are deterred by the effect which political instability is now increasingly having upon African universities. Financial cutbacks have damaged the environment within which research and teaching take place; military governments have answered student political militancy by repression, even gunfire; in some countries there are grave fears as to whether universities can survive as centres of free and critical enquiry. Since it is any case becoming increasingly difficult to finance, organize and implement long-term schemes of academic collaboration, the temptation is strong to leave African cousins to solve their own problems. Yet despite all the pessimism, academic links remain one of the strongest parts of the post-colonial relationship. The effects of university expansion in West Africa have been quite as far-reaching as the Elliot Commission expected, but considerably more complex and equivocal than those who engaged in it ever recognized.

It need not imply guilt or remorse to suggest that during the last thirty years British academics have accepted their assigned roles in the process of African "nation-building" a little too uncritically. Social scientists have been slow to apply to universities the sort of complex and critical cost-benefit analysis they find appropriate to other development projects, such as railways or agricultural enterprises, which raise immediate suspicions of economic self-interest. Past decisions are irretrievable, and future ones lie in other hands; but historians can always hope for retrospective wisdom. Elliot and his colleagues found it easy enough to see the beneficial effects which new colleges would bring:

> The diffusion of universally valid knowledge, as a key to power;
> The liberal education of wise statesmen;
> The formation of technically competent cadres;
> The generation of locally-relevant research and enquiry,

and to assume that these would justify the financial costs which they under-estimated so grossly. It would have required greater foresight, though it should not have been impossible, to foresee other consequences:

> The widening of income differentials among Africans;
> The magnetic drift of primary and secondary education towards the goal of university entrance;
> The costly errors which could result from faulty academic advice;
> The psychological stress and cultural alienation which some students would experience;
> The political impact of critically-minded student leadership;
> The heavy burden which recurrent costs would lay upon African tax-payers.

And perhaps it was not wholly unreasonable to discount as inevitable by-products the incidental advantages which might accrue to the foreigners employed in the enterprise:

> Opportunities for rewarding employment or travel;
> Contracts for building and equipment;

Markets for English-language monographs and textbooks (not to mention periodicals and novels and records and other cultural artefacts);
The invigorating enlargement of their own intellectual horizons.

Some future historian may eventually produce an assessment of academic decolonization sufficiently complex to comprehend all these costs and benefits, and even to evaluate them. Meanwhile it is at least a beginning to recognize their existence.

6 The Idea of a Colonial University

On 1 February 1971 one student of the University of Ibadan was killed, and several were injured, by police who had been called to the campus as a result of student demonstrations originating in allegations of corrupt administration in a hall of residence. The Vice-Chancellor, testifying before a judicial enquiry appointed by the head of state, remarked (with specific reference to the residential system) that the university structure at Ibadan remained "subcolonial".[1] His words were taken up, and given an interpretation which he had probably not intended, by a subsequent witness (a radical young sociology lecturer called Dr Onoge), who defined a colonial university as one which paid greater attention to its standing in the eyes of foreigners than to the relevance of its activities to the needs of its own country. Both men agreed that much of the framework within which their university operates had originated outside Nigeria; but whereas the Vice-Chancellor seemed to direct his criticism at relatively superficial aspects, such as physical facilities, his colleague was attacking intellectual assumptions of a more fundamental nature. It is manifestly true that Ibadan (and other universities in Africa and elsewhere) originated in a particular phase of British colonial policy; it may be salutary for British academics (who are often perspicacious in criticizing policies in which they are not personally involved) to consider how far these alien importations did, as was hoped, bring with them ideas and values of universal reference, and of specific applicability to the needs of twentieth-century Africa.

The origins of these universities may be found in the reports of two royal commissions—the Asquith and Elliot Commissions on Higher Education in, respectively, the colonies generally and West Africa specifically, which appeared in 1945.[2] At the time of their appointment the wartime coalition was formulating a whole new range of new strategies for the dependent colonies, designed to further the development of their resources, the promotion of public services which would increase the welfare of their people, and the gradual emergence of well-educated elites to whom the British government could gradually transfer responsibility for the administration, the technical services and (more slowly, perhaps) for the taking of political decisions. Within this strategy, the specific role of universities would be to educate men who (working in partnership with their colonial masters) would build up some of the structures needed for a modern liberal state, more or less in the British image— an honest administration, capable of utilizing modern science and technology to sink shafts of modernity deep into traditional African societies. In short, the foundation of such universities as Ibadan and Legon was part of a British strategy for gradual and controlled decolonization.

Some commentators are inclined to think that such policies originated only during the Second World War—emphasizing the damage done by that war to British political and economic strength, and the encouragement it gave to anti-imperialist forces generally, but notably in the two "super-powers" whose rivalries were to dominate the post-war world. In fact, the possibility of shaping society through educational policy has been recognized by both Europeans and Africans for over a century. Sir Eric Ashby has traced[3] the idea that the British government should found universities in its African colonies back to the 1870s. It was originally voiced by a small group of far-sighted African intellectuals (Blyden, Horton, James Johnson); and, although some British officials were wholly contemptuous of the idea, the general response of British officialdom was by no means unsympathetic in principle. But they did not believe that resources could be found to implement their sympathetic intentions, and—with one exception—little happened until the 1930s.

The exception was Fourah Bay College in Sierra Leone, founded by the Church Missionary Society in 1827, which became affiliated to Durham University in 1876, so that its students could be prepared for a BA degree (with a classical and theological bias), and for a Licentiate in Theology, without leaving African soil. Here already was an educational institution perceived as a leaven for the transformation of African society—although in this case the transforming agent was to be not the intellectual values of the academic community but the spiritual power of Protestant Christianity. I am not concerned to trace the successes and failures of this ideal, or the varied fortunes of the college as an institution. At the time of the Elliot Commission's visit it was reduced to a nucleus of six staff and 25 students, evacuated from Freetown to a cheerless isolated site in the Protectorate; still essentially a missionary college, staffed by dedicated men and women of liberal education, in whom religious motives took precedence over academic ones. (Some of these underpaid workers in the vineyard became my own colleagues in 1952, and I have the highest regard for their devotion.) The Commission found among African leaders (not least among the college's own alumni, three of whom were actually members of the Commission) a deep conviction that the educational aims of the founders could best be carried through if secularized; there was a strong demand that Fourah Bay should become a university college, its links with Durham strengthened. But I am afraid that up to that time the University of Durham had been little more conscious than other British universities of the opportunities and challenges available in Africa; and although it did more under the vice-chancellorship of Sir James Duff (a member of the Elliot Commission), that Commission did not regard Fourah Bay as a suitable nucleus from which there might develop the sort of colonial university that they had in mind.

The aims which such a university might pursue had been in process of formulation in and around the Colonial Office during two decades. In 1933 one departmental committee under Sir James Currie, a former Director of Education in the Sudan, had argued that institutions of "a real university standard" (as contrasted with existing institutions geared to vocational training) could help provide "that reasonable degree of social and economic security, without which there can be no solid or lasting basis for any real cultural life". Ten years later another committee under H. J. Channon—Professor of Biochemistry at Liverpool, and possibly the first British academic to address himself whole-heartedly to such problems—argued that, if his still largely apathetic colleagues in this country could be involved in what he envisaged as "the Colonial University", they could create "an acknowledged centre of learning which will act as the focus of the intellectual development of the territory".[4] But it is doubtful whether the funds necessary to realize these visions would have been provided but for the political impetus imparted by the Coalition government's Secretary of State, Oliver Stanley. To the idea of a greatly extended

British responsibility for colonial development, which had begun to affect many aspects of policy during the 1930s, Stanley added the injunction that it was necessary to commence preparation for colonial self-government, though even in West Africa this was seen as still lying many decades ahead. As a result of his contacts with Stanley, Channon gave prominence in his 1943 report to the British government's commitment "that the Colonies shall become increasingly self-governing as the degree of their development makes the carrying out of this policy possible", and as soon as his report was submitted Stanley approached British vice-chancellors to ask their co-operation in "quickening the progress of Colonial peoples towards a higher level of social well-being and towards the ultimate goal of self-government".[5]

Slowly and gradually, as university interest was aroused by the Asquith and Elliot reports, the indifference and widespread ignorance of British academics towards problems in African and Asian colonies was modified by the enthusiastic commitment of a few of them. But the work of building up colonial universities would never have received the necessary financial support had it not been linked with the political objective of preparing decolonization. To say that the inspiration was political does not mean that it was sinister or unworthy; the Elliot Report presented the objective in terms unusually eloquent for a royal commission:

> Somewhere in West Africa within a century, within half a century – and what is that in the life of a people? – a new African state will be born. It will be strong. Its voice will be listened for, wherever there are Africans or African-descended communities, and that is to say both in the Old World and in the New. It will have a vital need for counsellors, its own counsellors. Now is the time, and the time is already late, to train them for their work.[6]

And certainly the contribution which British universities were invited to make was one which seemed to require nobody to compromise his intellectual integrity: basically, it was to be the transmission and protection of academic standards which they sincerely believed to be universally valid and culture-free.[7]

Universally valid one is still entitled to think them, but culture-free they certainly were not. As Ashby shows, the intellectual values which these colleges set out to promote were directly related to a particular phase in the development of English Universities.[8] And of course it could not have been otherwise; if British academics had waited to act until they had freed themselves from the corrupting influence of their own history they would have waited for ever. The "Asquith colleges" might have been very much more unfortunate in their inheritance. All the same, it seems to me that if some of their sponsors had paused to consider the applicability of some of their own convictions we would think better, rather than worse, of their intellectual objectivity. Three particular assumptions may serve as examples.

First there was the assumption that universities had some responsibility for shaping moral as well as academic values within an "intellectual aristocracy". Essentially this is an "Oxbridge" assumption; Sir Walter Moberly's *The Crisis in the University* (published in 1949 and read by many teachers in the new colleges) is a thoughtful and humane discussion of how the values professed by Newman and Jowett could be preserved in large English "redbrick" universities, then embarking on their first post-war expansion. One does not however find, in Moberly or in the planning documents of the colleges, much discussion of the rather different educational goals of Scottish universities, nor of their possible relevance to the problems of providing intellectual direction in developing communities.

The second assumption was probably more strongly held in Redbrick itself, though it came originally from Germany: I mean the conviction that research is an essential function of any true university. This many of us *would* regard as universally valid; but it can easily change into the more dubious argument that research is *the* essential function of a university – not just that it is a necessary condition of effective teaching, but that it is more important than good teaching. Thus the second Principal of University College Ibadan could write (in a dull but often revealing book published in 1960) that "the most important development of all for any university institution is the development of a post-graduate school. It is on such a school that a university ultimately depends for its reputation."[9] Moreover, this argument did not always distinguish very carefully the various possible meanings of "research" in – say – physics, English literature and agriculture; it was often associated with a secondary assumption that "pure" or "fundamental" research always ranked higher than "applied" research, directed towards the solution of actual human problems.

Thirdly, there was the assumption that the quality of work done in a university depended on the maintenance of standards, which needed to be rigorously controlled by a system of external examinations.[10] In the 1940s, the very real threats to the quality of work in the new colleges could be seen from two quarters – from colonial administrations preoccupied with a legitimate but myopic concern with training men to fill immediate openings in government service, and from Africans eager to secure the social status and economic benefits which in colonial society attended upon the possession of university degrees. Alarmed by the two dreadful spectres of comical Indian degree-factories and of the controversial Higher College at Yaba,[11] the Elliot and Asquith Commissions sought to guarantee quality by binding the syllabus, examinations and general facilities of the new colleges to standards defined by the University of London – whose senate rose to the occasion by agreeing to work out terms for a new "special relationship". The maintenance of standards by external examination became a paramount concern upon which Colonial Office planners united with the local West African leadership. For British policy-makers, academic standards were guarantees for the quality of the ruling elites upon whom the future of African nations (and their relationship with the Commonwealth) would depend; African intellectuals had still more immediate interests at stake. Throughout the twentieth century they had been hindered from access to senior colonial appointments on the grounds that they lacked adequate qualifications; they were determined that no such pretext should debar their children. The fervent commitment of African opinion to the maintenance of externally-controlled standards as the hallmark of academic quality was not simply testimony to their faith in the wise and just senators of London University; it was itself a product of the colonial situation.[12]

The colonial universities, into which the Asquith colleges were to grow, were explicitly *not* intended to be carbon-copies of English models. But these governing assumptions of their founders did point towards the development of high-level, high-cost, institutions with standards determined externally. And under their early leaders, English standards were not only respected, but frequently improved upon.

This was true with regard to their physical environment. A great deal of thought, and a great deal more money than was originally intended, went into creating sites and buildings which would conduce to high thinking, though not (by the accustomed standards of most entrants) to plain living. Distinguished architects (notably Jane Drew and Maxwell Fry) laboured to produce genuine tropical equivalents to the dreaming spires of Oxford. This involved not merely good libraries and laboratories, but fountains, towers and dual carriage-ways. Unless the buildings as well as the academic standards could be an example to the country, wrote Ibadan's first Principal, "Nigerian public opinion, already sceptical, would give no support to the College".[13] And, as Professor Lambo correctly noted, residential accommodation was an essential part of the design – primarily, no doubt, because the private housing available in African cities at the time would not provide students with an environment conducive to high-level intellectual activity, but also because many British academics at the time believed that a collegiate or hall system was the most promising way to introduce into their own redbrick universities the elements of "a real community, diffusing a distinctive atmosphere which is morally and intellectually stimulating".[14]

It was true of their staffing. As all involved recognized, this was a crucial but extremely difficult problem. If the new colleges were to attract experienced scholars from established universities (rather than experienced schoolteachers looking for a change) they would have to offer, not merely competitive salaries and generous leave, but good facilities for research and favourable staffing ratios. (It was hoped that if favourable enough they would also encourage the development of tutorial work on Oxbridge lines; but discreet references in books by the first two principals of Ibadan suggest that this was not very successful,[15] and the system has not left much trace there today.) In many cases, though of course not in all, these provisions did attract dedicated and distinguished scholars, whose teaching and research was of inestimable value to what many of them came to regard as their adopted countries. But the price paid for this (somewhat uneven) quality of staff was that very costly standards of staffing were accepted as usual in the colonial universities; today, staff/student ratios still allow many university teachers more favourable research/teaching ratios than their colleagues in Britain.

Similar assumptions lay behind the development of the syllabus. Although the sponsors of the colonial universities were well aware that the countries for which they were planning would need many graduates with professional and applicable skills, their proposals for providing them were governed by this over-riding concern with academic standards. In engineering, where the Elliot Commission believed that most foreseeable openings would not require men with university training,[16] it was decided to leave development to the second string of the colonial "binary system" – the so-called CAST Colleges. In medicine on the other hand, the unhappy experience of students at Yaba – who spent six and a half years in acquiring a local qualification of sub-professional standard – gave a strong impetus to the demand for courses which could meet the rather rigorous requirements set by the British medical profession. To achieve their recognition the University of Ibadan had to initiate the building of a teaching hospital, at a cost to Nigeria of nearly £5 million, and to provide facilities on a scale which meant that it long remained more expensive to train a medical student in Nigeria than to send him to Britain. Ibadan now has a very good medical school and teaching hospital, which have of course brought considerable side-benefits to Nigerians – especially those who need specialized surgery and happen to live near Ibadan. But there is still quite fierce disagreement as to whether the range of medical studies then prescribed was really in accordance with Nigerian priorities. Today Ahmadu Bello and Ife Universities are developing syllabuses which not only place more emphasis on preventive medicine than on advanced surgical techniques, but base their teaching not on a single super-hospital but on a group of more modest (and more typical) ones.

Much of the early development in the colonial universities took place in basic sciences, and still more in arts. This was not merely because arts courses were less costly to begin, but because the sponsors had confidence in the capacity of an arts course to provide a liberal education through "a training in clear and objective thought and in appreciation of the accumulated wisdom of the outside world".[17] In practice they sought to do this through the specific types of arts course long established in England. Both Ibadan and Legon quickly developed notable classical departments; but, as Ashby notes, ten years after Ibadan was founded, "no courses were offered in engineering, economics, law, geology, anthropology, sociology, public administration or Arabic and Islamic studies, and it had taken eight years to establish a department of education".[18] Most of these deficiencies have since been made up, but the early pattern of studies is a crucial one for a new institution; the procedures, precedents and general tone of the academic boards were largely set up by professors of the subjects considered basic in English patterns of liberal education.

I do not imply, of course, that this is a bad pattern, or that it has proved incapable of adaptation to meet African needs. Many of the first teachers in the Asquith colleges have been pioneers in giving to teaching and research in their disciplines new orientations derived from the African environment. In my own subject, history, this process began quite early and has been carried on with increasing momentum by African scholars trained in the colleges, and historians throughout the world have learned much from their achievements. Yet even here, the necessity of "maintaining standards" by working through the special relationship with London tended to delay innovations; and I think progress was slower still in developing new syllabuses in social medicine, or in applying engineering sciences to the technological needs of developing societies.

Finally, English practice affected the approach of African universities to the recruitment of students. As an additional safeguard against any lowering of the standards of degrees, standards for entrance, expressed through certificate examinations, were also assimilated initially to those of London. Since opportunities to prepare adequately for these exams in Africa were thinly and unevenly spread, intakes of students remained small. Ibadan, which opened in 1948 with 104 students, had raised its total enrolment to 368 in 1952-3. In that year recurrent expenditure amounted to more than £410 000, or about £1114 a head; the college's total expenditure up to that time, capital and recurrent, was nearly £10 million, of which at least eight million came from Nigerian sources.[19] As the school system improved and African development proceeded, the colleges responded to demand by admitting less well-qualified applicants for preliminary studies; but they continued to give a very expensive education to this enlarged elite. In 1969-70, when the student population of Ibadan had risen to 3500, each student still required a recurrent expenditure by the university of £1174, of which £781 was provided directly by the Nigerian Treasury.

I am not suggesting that the planners of the Asquith colleges intended to promote any sort of neo-colonialism; on the contrary, their concern to apply their own working assumptions overseas testifies to their sincere belief in inter-racial equality. But these were not the only assumptions compatible with such a belief. When the University of Nigeria was founded at Nsukka in 1960, many people suggested that American land-grant colleges offered alternative practices and philosophies in some ways more relevant to African needs. Other possible alternatives might have been found nearer home; it is surprising that a commission presided over by a Glasgow graduate and former Rector of Aberdeen University should not have given more serious consideration to Scottish university models. In Scotland ancient universities, founded (in the words of Aberdeen's Papal Bull of Foundation) to bring a little culture and learning to the "rough, unlettered, and almost untamed" people of remote regions, were admitting as students a larger proportion of the population, drawn from a wider social base and with wider though less highly-specialized achievements in secondary school; and were giving them a broadly-based general education as a preliminary to specialized studies. However, this question was not asked, and the Asquith colleges developed as "academic counterparts of English university institutions".[20]

It would of course be absolutely wrong to suggest that no adaptation to African needs and African conditions took place; there was a great deal even during the period of affiliation to London and Durham, and exciting developments in this direction are continuing all the time. But the most striking success of the Asquith colleges was in fulfilling their primary role as "colonial universities"—in building up facilities for the education of an undergraduate elite, and for research work, by post-graduate students as well as by senior members. These successes, acclaimed by most African leaders, have also won international recognition. Foundations poured in money to reinforce their evident excellence—often creating new academic vested interests, in the shape of specialized institutes and small research-oriented departments, which the universities would eventually take over as prior claims on their budgets (and so on the tax-payers of their countries).

But there was no need for external pressure to maintain what a Nigerian commission of 1960 called "the intellectual gold standard";[21] the colonial university teachers, African and expatriate, gave this objective over-riding priority. The emerging pattern of arts degrees provides an excellent example of how their ideals interacted with external influences to press the idea of a colonial university, as one dedicated to the formation of a small nation-building elite, even further than the founders envisaged. The original Academic Board at Ibadan, later supported by a delegation from the Inter-University Council, echoed the traditional Scottish doctrine by saying that general degrees "establishing a broad basis of cultural and scientific education" should form the core of undergraduate teaching. But the London General BA (unlike the BSc) is something of a poor relation—a pass degree, which under colonial regulations carried lower salaries and lower status; and when Ibadan asked London whether it would be possible to raise the status by awarding honours on the basis of its examinations, they received the conventional English answer that a broad-based education could not be regarded as a proper academic discipline.[22] Not surprisingly, students and staff reacted by strongly favouring specialized honours courses on the London pattern, qualified only by patronizing references to the ordinary degree as "perhaps the best training for a schoolmaster".[23] Today in Ibadan and Ife the ordinary BA exists only as a shabby consolation prize awarded to candidates who have failed to reach the still jealously-guarded 'standards' of the honours schools, although many students of the ever-expanding intake would have been manifestly better served by a genuine general degree adapted from Scottish, American or even "plate-glass English" models. Here an aim of the founders seems to have been frustrated by the London affiliation which they had been so anxious to promote.

The Honours graduates have of course come forward too; but the new African elite of which they form a major part has tended to come under increasing attack – from disgruntled friends of Africa as well as from old enemies.[24] It is undeniable that this elite, among whom African academics are prominent, do enjoy incomes, including such "fringe benefits" as subsidized housing, car allowances, leave entitlements, which place their living standards many times above those of the mass of their countrymen. This however is not necessarily due to greed; it is an inevitable consequence of the policy of building African universities on the "intellectual gold standard". If conditions of service need to be attractive to recruit distinguished expatriates, how can local scholars be treated on a different basis? To imply general corruption or moral depravity on their part is grossly unfair; even if they were willing to accept low personal incomes, it would be a betrayal of their whole formation to accept libraries or laboratories inadequate to the tasks assigned to them. Though there are occasional distasteful displays of academic elitism, the weakness and strengths of African academics seem to me essentially the same as those of academics everywhere. I would not suggest that my colleagues in Ibadan, as a group, were either more or less materialistic or corrupt than my colleagues in Aberdeen. What I do say is that, in many of the African universities, the colonial legacies are becoming more, rather than less, apparent with the passage of time – not only the more obvious ones noted by Lambo, but the more profound ones noted by Onoge.

British academics who have been involved in building up universities in former colonies set themselves the job of promoting excellence – defined as the production of work which will be so recognized by the international community of scholars. They were right to do so – and could not have been involved in this work on any other terms. Scholars from other countries – especially USA – have recognized their achievements and hurried to join in themselves. Their own work has thereby been enriched. I am convinced that the benefits to British universities (to name no others) of their work for the colonial universities has far more than repaid the cost to them. And the same is true, in my own experience, of individuals.

You may remember the words of the psychiatrist in Conrad's *Heart of Darkness* who conducts Marlow's medical examination in Antwerp:

> I have a little theory which you Messieurs who go out there must help me to prove. This is my share in the advantage my country shall reap from the possession of such a magnificient dependency. The mere wealth I leave to others.

We scholars now find it more interesting – and quite safe – to go out ourselves to prove our little theories; but our share in the advantages is hardly diminished.

Africans too have of course already derived advantages from their new universities; and these will be increasingly widely shared as the universities continue to relate their teaching and research programmes to local needs. But the price has proved far heavier than those who conceived the vision of the colonial university expected. The Elliot Commission underestimated the initial costs of establishing Ibadan by about 90 per cent. As the first Principal commented, "Had the Nigerian authorities (in 1947) had any idea how much it was going to cost, it is unlikely that they would have consented to its creation."[25] The Nigerian authorities of today value their universities more highly than did their predecessors: but despite all the foreign aid which has flowed in, the financial liabilities which universities impose on African tax-payers continues to mount. In 1965–6 government subsidies to post-secondary education in Sierra Leone – though felt in the university to be at best barely adequate for the maintenance of international standards—amounted to 6 per cent of total national expenditure.[26]

There are social costs too. The effect of concentrating so high a proportion of national resources on the education of an intellectual elite – who, possessing qualifications on the "international gold standard", may expect to be remunerated on that standard – can in the short run only be to intensify inequalities and social tensions. And when academic qualifications carry expectation of material reward so far above the national average, it becomes proportionately even more difficult than elsewhere for students to conduct the pursuit of truth in a wholly disinterested way. I believe that the idea of a colonial university, and the attempt to give expression to it, represents one of the best achievements of British colonial policy. But, like all colonial legacies, it contains very serious problems for those inheritors. Outsiders who advise on its further development should never lose these from sight.

7 History: African and Contemporary

By a regrettable anomaly in our Association's practice,* now removed, two distinguished historians who preceded me in this office – Roland Oliver and John Fage – were never called upon to deliver Presidential Addresses. So, with the exception of our first President (Dame Margery Perham) – whose historical writing achieves a distinction which few of us can hope to emulate, but who has been so much else besides – I find myself the first historian to discharge this duty. I feel somewhat as Lepidus must have done when invited to speak on behalf of the Triumvirate.

I suppose I should begin by claiming – as I think I can justly do – that historians have played a distinctive and important part in the development of African Studies during the last quarter century, and in the affairs of our own young Association. But an unkind critic might reply that, since historians already occupied well-established positions within the European academic world before the second world war, they also bear responsibility for the relatively retarded status of African history in earlier years. And I must begin by admitting that such study *was* retarded.

During my own undergraduate studies in the distinguished Manchester History School, which I entered in 1940, I can hardly recall even a token recognition of the existence of tropical Africa. Our syllabus assumed that the Graeco-Roman world, and its heirs, were the centre of all historical developments worthy of, or indeed susceptible to, serious study. If our attention was ever drawn to any African or even Asian society, it was in the context of European imperial expansion. And within this Eurocentric syllabus the emphasis was heavily institutional – though Manchester, unlike some other departments, did require its students to look beyond politics and diplomacy and to undertake some serious study of economic organization.

* This was the ASAUK Presidential Address, September 1973

I must emphasize that my distinguished teachers, many of whom I was later privileged to call colleagues, were not illiberal or insensitive men, anxious to perpetuate colonialist myths of "peoples without history". This blind spot (as it seems to us) was actually a function of their intense professionalism. Historical studies had progressed above all by the rigorously critical study of documents; pre-colonial Africa, it was assumed, had generated no documents worth consideration; therefore African history could not be a serious subject of study. When in 1952 I announced my intention of resigning my lectureship at Manchester to work in Sierra Leone, Sir Lewis Namier (a very great historian who was himself deeply concerned with the historical experience of one of the "submerged peoples" of the world) was seriously distressed that I should sacrifice a promising career as an historian of European diplomacy in this way. (Shortly before his death in 1960 he somewhat reluctantly admitted that something had perhaps been salvaged from this shipwreck; "the wind of change is blowing in your direction," he wrote in the last letter I received from him.)

So much (you will be pleased to hear) for reminiscences. We can all recognize that things have now changed for the better. But this change is not simply a matter of new generations of historians, no longer blinkered by their own involvement in a colonialist society, feeling free to make public confession of the sins of their seniors. The growth of an academic tradition is always more complicated than that. Tonight I want to make a tentative attempt to show how the contribution which historians may claim to have made to the development of African Studies in this country might be related to changes in the methods and emphases of British historians generally, as well as to changes in our own historical environment.

But as I come to begin, I find this an appallingly complex task. When I try to summarize the lines along which historical studies have developed since the 1940s, I am reminded of Stephen Leacock's hero who leaped on his horse and rode off in all directions. Yet the cumulative effect of these developments does seem to have been to make professional historians less ill-equipped to approach the complexities of African material, and to engage in the multi-disciplinary studies which are the professed aim of Associations like our own.

First and most obviously there has been the territorial enlargement of the areas of study considered professionally acceptable, for teaching as well as for research. With this has gone some shift in attitudes towards different cultures – perhaps reflecting recognition of the work of anthropologists, perhaps just the decline of classical education – and this has weakened the single-minded attachment of historians to the world of the Graeco-Roman tradition. There is now more general interest in the history of societies as a whole, as against those ruling classes or elites who produced the most accessible documentation; this has entailed a shift towards sociological, demographic and cultural studies which require serious attempts to learn from and collaborate with other disciplines. (Not of course that this was a wholly *new* development; but the gap between pre-war British historians and their French colleagues may be gauged by comparing the reception given in 1944 to G. M. Trevelyan's chatty *English Social History* with the established achievements of Marc Bloch, Georges Lefebvre, and other distinguished members of the *Annales* school.) In recent years historians like E. P. Thompson, H. J. Dyos, Asa Briggs, have begun to ask, about the cities of the European Industrial Revolution, the sort of questions which have been engaging us today; with a few exceptions – and in view of my unfilial remarks about Manchester I must mention Arthur Redford's work on labour migration – few professional historians before the war would have thought these their concern. Clearly, such studies provide a better preparation for work on many problems of African history than a tradition which gives pre-eminence to constitutions and diplomacy.

These changes have been accompanied by a relaxation of self-imposed chronological limits. Undergraduate syllabuses no longer terminate in 1914, or even earlier; the Bulletin of the flourishing Association of Contemporary Historians records an ever-growing list of studies of mid-twentieth-century topics. There are difficulties in applying established methods of scholarship to contemporary subjects and these worry some historians. Known sources of vital evidence remain closed to researchers, and partisanship or ignorance may lead to the acceptance of positions which will later come to seem naive and misleading. Nevertheless, I am convinced that this extension has benefited the academic discipline of history in general, and in ways which have particular relevance to studies of Africa. Very briefly I would summarize three reasons for this:

(i) Deficiencies in archival material have obliged historians of the contemporary period – like those of earlier periods in Africa – to see what results they can achieve through the critical scrutiny of alternative sources of evidence.

(ii) Awareness that we are specially liable to incorporate our own biases in analyses of our own times may oblige historians to scrutinize their presuppositions about other subjects too more formally and directly.

(iii) Since in the twentieth century it has become evident that the history of every community is profoundly affected by events in distant continents, the practice of contemporary history may lead us to seek a more truly international perspective on earlier periods also.

In other words, the new status of contemporary history is not just a matter of changes in syllabuses and research techniques. It has reinforced the message of philosophers like Collingwood, that historians must think more carefully about the relationship between themselves, working in the library in the year 1973, and the evidence which permits them to make statements about the year 1873, or 873. Most historians have become more aware of the unity of past and present, in a way which has more in common with traditional African attitudes towards the past than with the sort of professionalized positivism which inspired the tradition of von Ranke. Good historical writing must certainly remain faithful to the past (by trying to understand, even to recreate, the thoughts and actions of men now dead in relation to the institutions, ideas and values of *their* society); but more scholars now recognize that it is also part of the present – "contemporary history", whatever the period studied – in that this operation can only be performed by men who are living in the world of 1973.

I think it is important that this dual nature should be understood, not only by professional historians, but by those who seek to incorporate historical evidence in their own studies of contemporary Africa. Most of us have experience of being asked to provide a short factual account of some great development, as if one could ransack the past like a magpie to find pieces to complete someone's personal jigsaw puzzle. We cannot provide a definitive and "factual" account of – say – the growth of Freetown or Ibadan, although we have professional criteria by which to judge particular statements true or false. But possibly our chief contribution may be to recall to social scientists the need to establish a precise historical context for any particular observation, whatever its date, from which they wish to draw general conclusions – a practice which may avoid the dangers of misapplying historical analogies.

For our view of the past has not become so relativist that we can regard it simply as a repository of tracts for the times; those who seek too freely for the "lessons" of history may fall into the error of projecting today's values into the minds of yesterday's men. Recently I discussed with a most distinguished pioneer of African studies the behaviour of those African rulers who during the 1880s actively assisted the installation of European power – by signing treaties, for example. My colleague could at first see no justification for them; we can now see that by this period the forces of European imperialism were gathering invincible strength, so such men must have been simple traitors. It was, he said, "like a Greek tragedy". Precisely. But the essence of Greek tragedy is that men do *not* understand the forces which shape their destiny. If Oedipus had *recognised* his parents, his story would be fit only for a horror comic. We can only understand his tragedy – and the tragedies of Samori, or Tofa of Porto Novo, or Edward Blyden – by understanding what problems they thought they were trying to solve; in Collingwood's controversial phrase, by re-enacting *their* thoughts in *our* minds.

When all has been said about the special aims and problems of this research project or that, the faithful re-interpretation of past experience in a language which can be meaningful to our own contemporaries seems to me the essential duty of the historian, whether he writes of Africa, Afghanistan or Aberdeen. It may involve laborious research, and present technical difficulties of limited interest; but if we cannot achieve such an understanding of past generations, how can we hope to achieve a perspective on the events of this year? Some scholars interpret the behaviour of this President, or that community, by reference to great historic forces in which they may be caught up; others concentrate on analysis of immediate problems to which their actions may be a response; those who succeed in doing both are, it seems to me, exercising the essential skills of the contemporary historian.

Many studies by social scientists do achieve some such perspective and what I am saying may already sound commonplace. If it does, I would venture to suggest that it is because historians have from the start been closely involved in the recent growth of African studies. But even if this claim is justified, I do not think they could have made such a contribution, or given a greater impetus to such work, at any earlier date. I do not see the first half of this century as a period when historians "missed the bus"; no service was running to

Africa in any case. "To every thing there is a season and a time to every purpose under heaven." If African studies *had* become academically established in this country during the inter-war period, our Association today would be a very different – and, I think, less flourishing – body.

This assertion is only partly based on the rudimentary analysis I have tried to give of how history – like every other discipline – has developed and matured in recent decades. For the whole historical context in which our studies take place has also changed. It is always salutary to follow one of these sermons on the theory of history with a little practice; so I would like to conclude by considering the case of the Centre of African Studies which was, finally, *not* established in the University of Oxford in 1930.

The outline of this story can now be traced in the Lothian Papers in the Scottish Record Office, and the initiative (like many other false starts in the history of the modern Commonwealth) came from that close group of imperial idealists associated with *The Round Table*. Specifically it came from Philip Kerr, 11th Marquess of Lothian. In 1925 Kerr became Secretary of the Rhodes Trust, which some of his associates in the famous "Moot" seem to have regarded as a talent entrusted to their collective stewardship, for the purpose of spreading the ideals and influence of a purified British Commonwealth in the sadly divided world of the twentieth century. From his service with Milner in South Africa, Kerr himself had retained a conviction that Africa would provide a critical test for British imperial statesmanship; more clearly than some of his colleagues, he saw that success would depend on achieving a more profound and scholarly understanding of the problems and needs of African populations. This study he believed could best be undertaken by Anglo-Saxons enlightened by the particular type of political wisdom and idealism which, as Rhodes himself believed, was pre-eminently found in the University of Oxford.

During the 1920s however some of the Rhodes trustees sensed that all was not well with modern studies at Oxford. As a friendly American critic put it, the University had perhaps "dropped out of some of the Main Currents of Modern Life" and was in danger of being out-distanced by LSE[1] – an institution associated with some very unsound ideas. At undergraduate level, an attempt to close the gap had recently been made with the institution of "Modern Greats", but Kerr's close collaborator Lionel Curtis in particular was anxious to back this up by establishing some School of advanced political studies. During the later 1920s there were evidently discussions of how the Rhodes Trust might support such a plan; and it began to make one modest constribution by sponsoring series of lectures in Rhodes House by eminent visitors from overseas.

During the autumn of 1929 General Smuts visited Oxford, and gave the lectures which were published in 1930 as *Africa and Some World Problems*. Kerr took advantage of his visit to arrange meetings between those whom he described as African experts and "people in Oxford whom it is important to interest in African problems".[2] During these consultations Smuts persuaded Kerr (and more reluctantly Curtis) to transform the idea of a School of Government into a proposal for a Centre of African Studies.

But once details were worked out this proposal proved too ambitious for the Rhodes Trust (with its prior commitment to the large-scale scholarship scheme) to take on directly. While offering £15 000 to provide accommodation in an extension of Rhodes House, they turned to the Rockefeller Foundation in search of the running costs of the scheme. (I will not labour the irony of Rhodes' heirs turning to Rockefeller's in order to consumate the work of empire-building.) By February 1930 Kerr was asking Rockefeller to pledge £10 000 a year to a specific scheme.[3] The Centre was to consist essentially of four research professors, and a director. The fields of the four professors were to be: Political Science, History and Sociology – "the humane political tradition"; Science – or rather the application of science, the mobilization of "every contribution which scientific discovery can make to the solution of African problems"; Economics; and finally and rather oddly, "the African himself". It is a useful historical exercise to consider exactly what might have been studied under each of these headings, and an interesting parlour game to speculate on who the four professors might have been. There was to be provision for staff travel; for research studentships; and, most important, for associating with the work of the Centre representatives of the colonial administrations of Britain, France and Belgium, of South Africa – also missionaries, businessmen, former administrators and other interested academics. Co-operation, between scholars and practical men as well as between professors of different disciplines, was essential to the proposal; and in this Kerr could justly claim that the scheme was ahead of its time:

I don't think that any concrete scheme has ever yet been put forward for preparing a survey of a great human problem by bringing under review through thorough qualified persons the four main fields of knowledge, namely political science, natural science, economics and anthropology, using these words in their widest significance. Hitherto research has been to a considerable extent conducted in water-tight compartments leaving the synthesis to be effected by individual writers in periodicals or books, journalists or politicians [4]

Yet this scheme, imaginative though it was, did inevitably reflect assumptions of 1930 which would have limited the long-term usefulness of the Centre and weighed heavily upon the future development of African Studies in this country. Drawing its strength from the vigorous idealism of the Moot, it would have suffered from the limitation of their outlook. Since they accepted the long-term continuance of European rule in Africa as both beneficent and necessary, the Centre was intended to permeate the rulers with their ideas and ideals. Far from detaching itself from the processes of colonial administration, the Centre would have been deliberately involved in continuous dialogue with colonial administrators and policy-makers, following the model which Curtis had helped to develop at Chatham House. Reginald Coupland (then Beit Professor, a man whom Kerr at least may have expected to play a formative role) complained that H.A.L. Fisher envisaged the Centre *too much* as an agency for the commissioning of research, "which is to mind quite subordinate to the idea of a 'Fellowship' of all men co-operating in building up a new body of knowledge and inspiring research in all directions."[5] Research so inspired could only have been carried out in close collaboration with those members of the "Fellowship" who were themselves engaged in governing colonies.

We can see what difficulties this would have involved by reference to the views of Kerr's predecessor at the Rhodes Trust, Sir Edward Grigg, then Governor of Kenya. Having reluctantly facilitated the researches in which Margery Perham had been sponsored by the Trust, Grigg complained bitterly "that Rhodes's money should be spent on people who arrive in Africa with ready-made opinions and return to England to defeat the most cherished of his aims".[6] He would clearly have been most unwilling to accept further research workers whose ready-made opinions did not coincide with those of colonial administrators. Kerr, who had a far broader view of what scholarship involved, vigorously defended the principle of "diversity of opinion", adding that Miss Perham's work "would be beneficial to Oxford which still tends to take its views ready-made from the past".[7]

But there would have been continuing pressure to make research the servant of administration. This attitude is reflected in Kerr's relations with Thomas Jesse Jones, a fellow patron of African Studies: Jones felt that R. L. Buell's pioneer survey departed so far from the viewpoint of men actually dealing with African problems as to "border closely on propaganda".[8] In February 1930, Kerr apparently told Jones that the two bases of the Centre's work would be: (i) English political experience and study; (ii) American economic and sociological interest; and Jones took this to mean that the professor of "the African himself" would be no armchair anthropologist but a Jeanes School practitioner like J.W.C. Dougall.[9] I think Jones may have been mistaken – there are indications that, on the advice of J. H. Oldham, Kerr came to think seriously of Radcliffe-Brown[10] but in the context of the period, such an appointment was perfectly conceivable.

Kerr and his closer associates certainly knew that scholarship could not be subordinated to short-term administrative expediency; but it could have been no part of their aim to dissociate research from the goals of colonial administrators. Indeed – as Smuts' role suggests – much of the inspiration of this scheme came from their continuing faith in the creative capacities of South African liberalism. (Sometimes indeed the scheme was described as a *South African Institute.*)[11] Kerr's own attitude to future relations between the Union and the East African colonies seems to have been rather complex; but he feared that his basic objective of "confident cooperation between the white man at home and the white man on the spot" would be threatened by any overt confrontation between the doctrine of the paramountcy of African interests and the actual interests of white settlers.[12] As a political strategy for 1930, Kerr's views seem shrewd and relatively enlightened; but they implied some express and self-imposed restriction of the problems to be tackled within an organized research programme. When Kerr complained about scholars expressing "a very definite political view of Africa", he was not thinking of the impassioned argument in Smuts' Oxford lectures, for intensified white settlement as a means to the speedy civilization of Africans, but of a protest by Norman Leys, Josiah Wedgwood, Lancelot Hogben and others against a

B.B.C. publication which seemes to imply "a fundamental difference of mentality between Africans and Europeans".[13] The success of the Centre might thus have come to depend on the partial proscription of propositions which in this Association today we would hold to be fundamental.

A well-founded fear of becoming involved in "controversial political questions" was thus one reason why the Rockfeller Foundation decided not to support the scheme in 1930;[14] but only one. Faced as always with a choice of well-argued propositions they preferred to support the development of the International African Institute, which Malinowski persuaded them was the body best fitted to promote anthropological studies in Great Britain.[15] Without losing interest in the Oxford scheme, they wisely suggested that the research priorities of the proposed Centre required closer definition. After a select and high-powered luncheon meeting at Chatham House in May 1931, with Baldwin in the chair, the Carnegie Corporation of New York agreed to finance a general survey of African problems over a period of two years, in the hope that Rockefeller might later follow this up by accepting responsibility for some more permanent Institute.[16] There was some difficulty in finding an acceptable person to undertake this Survey; ultimately of course the choice fell upon Lord Hailey.

It is no part of my purpose today to appraise the remarkable *Survey* which Hailey eventually provided, except to say that it laid a more serviceable foundation for future studies of Africa than a full-scale Centre could have provided at that time. Had that come into being, African Studies in this country would have been associated with attitudes, goals and policies which were already becoming vulnerable, and placed in the hands of persons who would have found it difficult to win the confidence of post-war generations of Africans. Hailey's *Survey* on the other hand not only provided signposts and stimuli to enquiry and problem-oriented research in all sorts of directions, but exercised a substantial liberalizing effect on official policy; and it achieved this without creating a powerful new institution which would inevitably have laid the dead hand of obsolescent attitudes on the work which the post-war generation of scholars would perceive needed to be done.

I do not believe in ending on notes of complacency; so let me risk committing the terrible sin of moralizing. We should not think that our generation is any better equipped than Kerr's to stand outside history; *our* hands will one day be dead hands, and will seem to lie heavily on something or other. Some future Presidential address will doubtless consider how the work of our Association, founded in the first years of African independence by scholars largely trained during the period of decolonization, reflects the intellectual and political trends (in both strong and weak senses of that word) of the 1960s. What will it identify as *our* greatest weaknesses? Just conceivably, excessive detachment from the continent we study – an over-prim assumption that the results of the studies by which we make our professional reputations must automatically benefit peoples towards whom our government has already discharged its direct political responsibility. Avuncularism, I have often felt, is the highest form of paternalism. But perhaps when in our conference next year we consider the impact of Europe upon Africa we may see a little more clearly just where we ourselves stand within that continuing relationship.*

* I am not sure that this conference was quite so helpful in this respect as I hoped. But the attempt continues.

Notes

PREFACE

1. See our respective papers in L. H. Gann and P. Duignan (eds), *Colonialism in Africa*, Vol. 1, *The History and Politics of Colonialism, 1870–1914* (Cambridge, 1969).
2. Ronald Robinson, "Non-European foundations of European imperialism: sketch for a theory of collaboration", in Roger Owen and Bob Sutcliffe (eds), *Studies in the Theory of Imperialism* (1972), p. 133.
3. John D. Hargreaves, *Prelude to the Partition of West Africa* (1963), p. 182.

CHAPTER 1

1. *Encyclopaedia of the Social Sciences*, VII (1932), p. 613 s.v. Imperialism. 'Decolonization' does not appear in the Oxford Dictionaries (except in the *Supplement* published in 1972), nor the 1974 edition of the *Encyclopaedia Britannica*.
2. Governor Sir Hugh Clifford, Address to Nigerian Council, 29 December 1920.
3. T. N. Tamuno, "Governor Clifford and Representative Government", *Journal, Historical Society of Nigeria*, IV, i, December 1967.
4. E. A. Ayandele, *The Educated Elite in the Modern Nigerian Society* (Ibadan, 1974); N. Azikiwe, *My Odyssey* (1970), pp. 266–85.
5. *Journal Officiel*, Assemblée Nationale Constituante II, September 19th, 20th, 1946; for trans. extracts, J. D. Hargreaves, *France & West Africa* (1969), pp. 260–66.
6. Colonial No. 248, Report . . . by the Committee on Constitutional Reform (Coussey), 1949.
7. H. Foot, *A Start in Freedom* (1964), p. 109.
8. F. Fanon, *The Wretched of the Earth* (1961, Penguin ed., 1967), p. 27.
9. John Ballard, "The Porto Novo Incidents of 1923: Politics in the Colonial Era", *Odu*, II, 1965, pp. 52–75.
10. A. G. Hopkins, *An Economic History of West Africa* (1973), Chap. 7.
11. Parliamentary Papers, 1944–5, VI, Cmd 6607, Chap. I, para 17.
12. Cf. W. R. Louis, "Colonial Appeasement, 1936–1938", *Revue Belge de Philologie et d'Histoire*, XLIX, 1971, pp. 1175–91.
13. For the application of this concept to the study of British foreign policy, see D. C. Watt, *Personalities and Policies* (1965), esp. Chap. 1.
14. *Native Administration and Political Development in British Tropical Africa*, confidentially printed, 1942; cf. Hailey, *Native Administration in the British African Territories*, 5 vols, HMSO, 1950–53.

15. W. Roger Louis, *Imperialism at Bay: The United States and the Decolonization of the British Empire, 1941–1945* (1977)
16. Speech by Sir Stafford Cripps to the African Governors' conference, November 12th, 1947.
17. In an address to the Fabian Colonial Bureau of 14 December 1946, published by the Bureau under the title *Labour's Colonial Policy*.
18. Parliamentary Papers, 1944–5, V, Cmd 6655, p. 18. See also Eric Ashby with Mary Anderson, *Universities; British, Indian, African* (1966).
19. W. B. Cohen, *Rulers of Empire* (Stanford, 1971), pp. 176–9, 188–9.
20. *Soil Conservation and Land Use*, Government Printer, Freetown, Sessional Paper No. 1 of 1951.

CHAPTER 2

1. On this see J. M. Lee, "'Forward thinking' and war: The Colonial Office during the 1940s", *Journal of Imperial and Commonwealth History*, VI, 1977, pp. 64–79.
2. Hailey, *An African Survey* (1938), pp. 529, 537–42, 1639.
3. CO267/679/32097, Blood to Moyne, 110, 30 April 1941; cf below p. 58.
4. Jarle Simensen, "Commoners, Chiefs and Colonial Government; British Policy and Local Politics in Akim Abuakwa", Ph.D. thesis, University of Trondheim, 1976, II, pp. 297–302 and *passim*.
5. MacDonald to West African Governors, 18 December 1939, quoted in CO847/21/47100/1/1941. The wording to East African Governors was slightly different, and that to Central Africa referred to conversations with Huggins "as to the possibility of co-ordinating native policy in Southern Rhodesia, Northern Rhodesia and Nyasaland".
6. The agenda (revised in April 1942) and records of four early meetings are in C.O.967/13.
7. Quotations from Chapter I of this report [*NAPD*] which was confidentially printed in 1942, but submitted in cyclostyled form in March 1941 (C.O.847/21/37100/1).
8. Cf. this sentence, deleted at Burns's suggestion before the printing of Hailey's Report on the Gold Coast: ". . . when dealing with such questions as the extent to which electoral systems should be introduced into the townships, due weight should be given to the consideration that a broad policy of concessions in local government may make it easier for the Government to feel its way with some caution in planning constitutional changes." C.O.847/22/47100/9.
9. C.O.847/21/47100/1/1941 – Note of Hailey's discussion with Moyne and others, 18 March 1941.
10. On the question of publication and circulation, see C.O.847/21/47100/1/1942, 1943.
11. His interesting autobiography, *Colonial Civil Servant* (London, 1949) does not seem to do full justice to his readiness to innovate within the limits of current assumptions.
12. C.O.96/770/31013/5/1943, Minute by Gater on Williams draft of 20 January 1943; C.O.96/774/31336, Minute by Dawe, 5 June 1943.
13. Alan Burns and Robert Gardiner, *Other People, Other Ways*. Some suggestions to

Africans and Europeans visiting one another's countries (London 1950).
14. E.g. C.O.96/770/31032, Burns to Parkinson, 24 January 1942, refusing to allow the Director of Education power to close African schools – "to my mind the liberty of the subject (even the African subject) is of more importance even than education"; C.O.96/776/31486, Burns to Williams, 29 June 1943.
15. C.O.96/775/31444. Minutes by Burns, 22 September, by Williams 24 September: Record of discussion with Moyne, 30 September 1944.
16. C.O.96/774/31312; *Colonial Civil Servant*, pp. 186–8.
17. C.O.96/776/31466, Burns to Stanley, Conf. 17 December 1942 and minutes.
18. C.O.96/774/31336, Burns to Cranborne, 219 and Conf. 28 July 1942. It is interesting to compare Burns's stand against residential segregation on this extremely interesting file with his readiness to defend segregated clubs in print in 1949 (*Colonial Civil Servant*, pp. 58–9).
19. The episode is documented in C.O.554/131/33701/42; quotations from Burns to Cranborne, Secret, 30 June 1942; cf. *Colonial Civil Servant*, pp. 194–6.
20. C.O.96/770/31013/5, Burns to Stanley, Tel. 14 December 1942 and minutes.
21. C.O.554/131/33696/1942, Swinton to Cranborne, Pte. 13 October 1942. Cranborne to Burns and Stevenson, Tel. 6 December 1942.
22. *Colonial Civil Servant*, p. 69.
23. Jarle Simensen, *Akim Abuakwa* ..., pp. 301–6.
24. C.O.96/773/31229/6 Burns to Cranborne, Conf. 29 July 1942: Burns to Williams, Pte. 29 December 1942.
25. *NAPD* p. 138; C.O.96/772/31096/6, Burns to Stanley, Secret, 14 February 1943.
26. C.O.96/770/31013/5, Williams to Burns, 20 January 1943.
27. C.O.554/132/33718/4, Planned policy for West Africa; appointment of Development Adviser. Memo by Williams, Minutes by Dawe, 9 February, Stanley, 19 February 1943.
28. C.O.96/776/31475, Economic Policy in West African Colonies: Memorandum by Swinton, 24 February 1943.
29. C.O.554/132/33727, Copy of Minute by Swinton, 14 July 1943.
30. C.O.847/22/47100/8/1942, Cranborne to Stevenson, Conf. 18 August 1942.
31. C.O.847/21/47029/1942, Minute by Dawe, 15 May 1942; Stanley to Harlech. December 1942.
32. C.O.554/132/33718/4, Memo by Williams, February 1943.
33. C.O.554/132/33727, Note by Williams on "Constitutional Development in West Africa"; Note of meeting in Secretary of State's room, 20 July 1943. For earlier discussions on unofficial majorities, see C.O.96/31013/5, Minutes on Burns Tel. 14 December 1942.
34. *Ibid*. Minute by Williams, 4 September 1943; cf. Grantham to Stanley, 11 October 1943.
35. C.O.96/782/31499/1, Burns to Stanley, Secret, 4 October 1943, enclosing Petition.
36. C.O.96/770/31013/5, Burns Tel. 31 August 1943. C.O.96/776/31499, Burns to Stanley, Secret 5, 7, 8 October 1943; cf. *Colonial Civil Servant*, pp. 282–4.
37. C.O.96/31013/5, Minutes by Williams, 1, 6 September 1943, Stanley to Burns, Tel. 6 September 1943.
38. *Ibid*: Minute by Williams, 22 October: Note of Discussions with Stanley, 27–8

October 1943. C.O.96/776/31499, Minutes by Cohen 29 November, Seel 30 November, Gater 1 December 1943.
39. Burns's original proposals are evident in Burns to Stanley. Secret, 7 October 1943. (C.O.96/776/31499). The discussions with Stanley in May 1944 are documented in C.O.96/782/31499/1944.
40. C.O. 96/782/31499/1944, Minutes by Creasy, 16 September, Stanley 20 September 1944.
41. M. Wight, *The Gold Coast Legislative Council* (1947) pp. 202–206. Wight also provides a convenient contemporary study of the emergence of the new constitution.
42. C.O. 847/22/47160/10/1942, Memo by Adams 29 August 1942.
43. C.O. 847/21/47100/1/1943, Printed comments by Bourdillon on Hailey's general report.
44. *NAPD* p. 175: Bourdillon, "A Further Memorandum on the Future Political Development of Nigeria", (Confidential Print, Lagos, October 1942). C.O. 847/22/47100/10/1943, Memo by Bourdillon, 30 August 1943.
45. C.O. 554/132/33727, Note of Meeting, 19 November 1943.
46. CO. 267/683/32375, Notes of talks with Sir H. Stevenson, 16 July, 12 August 1943.
47. See Chapter 3.
48. C.O. 267/688/32348, Part II, Minute by Varwill, 22 November 1945.
49. See the introductory chapter by D. A. Low and J. M. Lonsdale in *The Oxford History of East Africa* (ed. D. A. Low and A. Smith) Vol. III (1976), esp. pp. 2–3.
50. Study of this interesting topic might begin in C.O. 554/139/33768 and in C.O. 554/140/33829/1.
51. C.O. 96/776/31499, Minute by Seel, 30 November 1943.
52. Paul Addison, *The Road to 1945: British Politics and the Second World War* (1975), p. 43.
53. *Ibid* pp. 233–4.
54. As Under-Secretary in 1945–46 Creech Jones devoted much effort to trying to force through the Minority Report of the Elliot Committee, which he had signed. This document was strongly favoured by the educational technocrats; it was the logical conclusion of their working assumptions about the supply of staff, students and finance, all of which subsequently proved erroneous. Its acceptance would have involved ignoring the deep attachment of Africans in the Gold Coast and Sierra Leone to existing institutions which, whatever their deficiencies, were living concerns with real assets. Czech Jones was far slower than many officials to recognize the force of these political considerations. See his minutes and comments in C.O. 554/134/33599 and C.O. 554/135/33599/1.
55. *Labour's Colonial Policy*. A Survey by Mr. Arthur Creech Jones M.P. Secretary of State for the Colonies. Fabian Colonial Bureau, 1947.
56. C.O. 554/135/33599/4/1946.
57. His Bellagio paper however gives a slightly misleading impression of the memoranda of May 1947 (which may be found in C.O. 847/36/47238). These interesting documents become available only after this chapter was completed, and have not yet been fully studied.
58. Report of the Committee of Enquiry into Disturbances in the Gold Coast. Colonial No. 231, 1948. p. 85.

59. Anthony Short, *The Communist Insurrection in Malaya, 1948–1960* (1975), pp. 27, 44–7, 80ff.
60. Colonial No. 231, pp. 17–20, 91–94; Hansard, 5th series, Vol. 448, Commons 1 March 1948. 37–8.
61. Speech by Montgomery to conference of African Legislative Councillors, 4 October 1948: J. B. Danquah's circular letter, 8 November 1948, in H. K. Akyeampong (ed), *Journey to Independence and After I*, (Accra, 1970), pp. 87–9.
62. Indian analogies were certainly drawn by the Chief Secretary, newly-arrived from the ICS. Reginald Saloway, "The new Gold Coast", *International Affairs* XXXI, 1955. pp. 469–76.
63. *Report of the Commission of Enquiry into the Disorders in the Eastern Provinces of Nigeria*, Nov. 1949. Colonial No. 256 of 1950. Hugh Foot, *A Start in Freedom* (1964), pp. 103–6; cf. above, p. 19.
64. The indispensable account of events in the Gold Coast remains Dennis Austin, *Politics in Ghana, 1946–60* (1964).
65. Creech Jones Papers, Rhodes House Oxford. (Mss. Br. Emp. S. 332) Box 18, File 4, fo. 32–4. C.O. Note on Constitutional Proposals, 15 October 1949. The guide to the official papers in Box 55, still closed, shows that the Cabinet discussed the Gold Coast on 13 October 1949.
66. Colonial No 250. Statement by H. M. Government. Creech Jones to Arden-Clarke 14 October 1949, p. 9; cf L. B. Namier, *Monarchy and the Party System*, Romanes Lecture, Oxford, 1952.
67. A. Creech Jones, "British Colonial Policy with particular reference to Africa", *International Affairs xxvii*, April 1951, p. 117.
68. The interaction between economics and politics during the period clearly requires fuller discussion than it receives here; for a beginning, see A. G. Hopkins, *An Economic History of West Africa* (1973), pp. 267–92.
69. P.P. 1957–58, IX, Cmnd 505, Nigeria: Report of the Commission appointed to enquire into the fears of Minorities and the means of allaying them. July 1958.

CHAPTER 3

1. J. F. Ade Ajayi, "The continuity of African institutions under colonialism" in T. O. Ranger (ed.), *Emerging Themes of African History* (1968), p. 194.
2. K. E. Robinson, *The Dilemmas of Trusteeship* (1965), p. 7.
3. CO 554/132/33727, Note on "Constitutional Development in West Africa".
4. On Creole history generally, see John Peterson, *Province of Freetown* (1961); L. Spitzer, *The Creoles of Sierra Leone* (Madison, 1974); A. T. Porter, *Creoledom* (1963). All these important studies derive initially from the fundamental work of Christopher Fyfe.
5. See J. A. Langley, *Pan-Africanism and Nationalism in West Africa, 1900–1945* (Oxford 1973), pp. 153–63.
6. CO 267/667/32010/1, Jardine to MacDonald, *Confidential*, 12 September 1939.
7. *West Africa*, 20 October 1945, enclosed in CO 267/688/32348, Pt. II.
8. See the introduction to the second edition of *Journey without Maps*.
9. CO 267/670/32210/2, Jardine to Dawe, 1 June 1939.
10. CO 267/682/32303, Minute on Fenton to Lloyd, Secret, 29 January 1941; CO 267/676/32216, Minute on Jardine to MacDonald, Secret, 25 April 1940.
11. M. McCall, "Kai Londo's Luawa and British Rule" (D. Phil. thesis,

University of York 1974) emphasizes the limited impact of colonial rule upon one area.
12. M. H. Y. Kaniki, "The Economic and Social History of Sierra Leone, 1929–1939" (Ph.D. thesis, University of Birmingham, 1972).
13. Kaniki, *op. cit.*, Chapter VIII; Spitzer, *op.cit.*, Chap. VI. His career is the subject of a Ph.D. thesis by La Ray Denzer of Birmingham University (1977).
14. For reference to his Communist associations, see E. T. Wilson, *Russia and Black Africa before World War II* (N. Y. 1974), especially pp. 243–53. Wilson relies heavily on references to Intelligence reports about alleged Communist contacts; until the evidence on which these were based is directly available it seems advisable to treat them with reserve.
15. F.C.B. Box 86, File 2, ff. 1–3, Wallace-Johnson to Padmore, 27 December 1939. CO 267/682/32303/42, Wallace-Johnson to Padmore, 25 May 1942, encl. in Stevenson to Cranborne, Secret, 12 March 1943. CO 267/683/32303/43, Wallace-Johnson to Brockway 16 February 1943 (in Beetham to Stanley, Secret, 12 March 1943).
16. CO 267/666/32215, Note by Williams, 1 September 1938.
17. CO 267/671/32245, Jardine-Dawe conversation, 17 January 1939. Communism is not mentioned in the Attorney-General's memorandum justifying Wallace-Johnson's detention on the outbreak of war – enclosed in CO 267/670/32210/2 Part II, Jardine to MacDonald, Secret, 23 September 1939. Also see CO 267/673/3254/3/39, Note by Williams, November 1939; Spitzer, *op. cit.*, pp. 200–1.
18. C. K. Meek, W. M. Macmillan and E. R. J. Hussey, *Europe and West Africa* (1940), pp. 76–7; Kaniki, *op. cit.*, pp. 328–9, 334, 352–3.
19. CO 267/667/32032, Sherbro Judicial District Legislation.
20. CO 267/672/32248, Native Taxation. The phrase quoted is from Jardine's address to the 1939–40 session of the Legislative Council.
21. CO 267/665/32208, Jardine to MacDonald, Secret, 30 June 1938.
22. Spitzer, *op. cit.*, pp. 190–1; the episode is documented in CO 267/665/32210.
23. CO 267/670/32199, Blood to MacDonald, Conf., 14 June 1939, encl. Stocks, 9 June.
24. CO 267/667/32032/39, Minutes by Williams, Bushe, January 1939; Dawe-Jardine conversation 17 January.
25. CO 267/670/32210/2 (Part 1), Blood to MacDonald, Secret, 8 February 1939.
26. CO 267/670/32210 (Part 2), Blood to Dawe, 15 March 1939.
27. CO 267/670/32210/2 (Part 1), Jardine to Dawe, 1 June 1939. Correspondence regarding the Ordinances, and texts of Legislative Council debates, are in CO 267/672–3/32254 and related files.
28. CO 267/673/32275, Blood to MacDonald, Conf., 22 August 1939; CO 267/671/32220; CO 167/673/32254/8, Brief by Williams, November 1939. On labour policy generally see H. E. Conway, "Industrial Relations in Sierra Leone with Special Reference to the Development and Functioning of Bargaining Machinery since 1945" (Ph.D. thesis, University of London, 1968).
29. See P.P. 1940–1, iv, Cmd 6277, *Labour Conditions in West Africa: Report by Major Orde-Browne*.
30. *NAPD*, pp. 12, 63–4, 81–2.
31. Cf. F. D. Lugard, *The Dual Mandate* (1929 ed.), pp. 85–6.

Notes to Chapter 3, pp. 58–63   129

32. *NAPD*, pp. 64–8.
33. This account is based on *NAPD*, pp. 69–83 and on CO 267/679/32097, Blood to Moyne, 110, 30 April 1941.
34. CO 267/679/32097, Blood to Dawe, 1 May 1941.
35. *Ibid.*, Stevenson to Cranborne, 75, 23 March 1942.
36. CO 267/679/32097, Minute by Cox, 29 November 1941.
37. CO 267/675/32120/2, Minute by Webber on Jardine to Lloyd, Conf. 24 June 1940.
38. CO 554/131/33696/42, Cranborne to Burns and Stevenson, Tel., 6 December 1942.
39. CO 267/674/32036, Jardine to MacDonald, 752, 11 December 1939 and encls.
40. CO 267/678/32203, Moyne to Stevenson, 256, 23 December 1941; CO 267/678/32036/2, Ramage to Stanley, 226, 8 October 1943.
41. CO 267/684/32036/2, Memo by Advisory Committee, 25 May 1944.
42. CO 267/678/32036/1, Education Department Scholarship Scheme. A list of holders is in CO 267/687/32303/2.
43. CO 267/667/32035 contains a copy of the Commission's Report (Colonial No 169).
44. CO 267/683/32354, Minute by Williams, 26 July, on Stevenson to Cranborne, 152, 27 June 1942; cf. his Minute of 24 July in CO 554/131/33702/42.
45. CO 554/131/33702/42, Stevenson to Cranborne, Tel., 27 October 1942; 25 March 1943.
46. CO 267/683/32375, Notes of talks with Sir H. Stevenson, 16 July, 12 August 1943.
47. CO 267/688/32348, Part 1. Sessional Paper No. 4, 1944, *Reconstitution of the Freetown City Council*; Stevenson to Stanley, Conf., 28 February, 1945, enclosing draft Bill.
48. For background to this, M. P. Banton, *West African City* (1957), Part One.
49. CO 267/688/32348, Part 1, Minute by Williams, 17 March 1945.
50. CO 267/688/32348, Part 2, Minute by Varwill, 22 November 1945.
51. For early signs of such tension, and Jardine's response, see CO 267/673/32285, Jardine to Dawe, Personal and Secret, 15 October 1939; CO 267/677/32319, Jardine to Williams, 9 October 1940, Note by Williams, 7 November; CO 267/682/32303, Minute by Williams, 1 February 1941.
52. For the growing opposition, and samples of press comment, CO 267/688/32348, Part 1; also CO 267/690/32397/1, Memo by Mayhew, 5 January 1945.
53. CO 267/688/32348, Part 1, Minutes by Creech-Jones, 28 August, 5 September 1945.
54. *Daily Guardian*, 19 February 1946, enclosed in CO 267/688/32348, Part 2, Stevenson to Gater, Secret, 5 March 1946, cf. Wallace-Johnson to CO, 2 November, 27 December 1945, *ibid*.
55. CO 267/688/32348, Part 1, Ramage to Hall, Conf. 29 August 1945.
56. See above, p. 34.
57. CO 267/684/32009, Ramage to Stanley, Secret, 16 June 1945.
58. CO 267/684/32010, Stevenson, Tel. 7 November 1944, Minute by Williams, 10 November.
59. J. R. Cartwright, *Politics in Sierra Leone 1947–1967* (Toronto, 1970); M. Kilson, *Political Change in an African State: A Study of the Modernisation Process in Sierra Leone* (Cambridge, Mass., 1966).

60. *F.C.B.*, Box 86, File 1A, R. B. Kowa to K. Little, 17 January 1948.
61. H. Foot, *A Start in Freedom* (1964) p. 15–a theme which Lord Caradon developed in his unpublished Callander lectures in the University of Aberdeen in 1975.
62. On the general direction of policy, see P.P. 1940–41, IV. Cmd. 6277, Labour Conditions in West Africa: Report by Major Orde-Browne. For reference to Nisbet's appointment, cf. above p. 57.
63. CO 267/681/32220 (Labour Department) includes a copy of CO Circular Telegram, 7 February 1941.
64. H. E. Conway, "Industrial Relations in Sierra Leone . . ." (Ph.D. thesis, London 1968).
65. CO 267/680/32199/2/43, Ramage to Stanley, Tel., 15 September 1943; Minute by Orde-Browne, 30 August, quoting Stevenson.
66. *F.C.B.* Box 86, File 2, fo. 118–9, Parry to Hinden, 29 December 1945.
67. *Ibid.* fo. 125–7, Parry to Hinden, 24 November 1946; fo. 128, Hinden to Parry, 24 December.
68. *Ibid.* fo. 130–1, Parry to Hinden, 9 February 1947.
69. *Ibid.* fo. 113–6, Parry to Hinden, 23 September 1945.
70. *Ibid.*
71. *Ibid.* fo. 118–9, Parry to Hinden, 24 December 1945.
72. *F.C.B.* Box 86, File 1A, Item 7, SLTUC *Statement on the Present situation in the Congress*; File 1B, fo. 111–4, Stevens to Nicholson, 15 May 1948. The WAFTU meeting is not discussed in the standard works on trade unionism in West Africa; for an attempt to follow it by a meeting in Dakar, which Stevens also attended, see W. Ananaba, *The Trade Union Movement in Nigeria* (1969), pp. 43, 91; I. Davies, *African Trade Unionism* (Harmondsworth 1966), p. 190.
73. *F.C.B.* Box 86, File 2, fo. 125–7, Parry to Hinden, 24 November 1946.
74. *Ibid.* fo. 134–5, Parry to Hinden, 16 March 1947; fo. 136–7, Parry to Hinden, 18 May 1947.
75. *Ibid.* fo. 125–7, Parry to Hinden, 24 November 1946.
76. *Ibid.* fo. 203–4, Stevens to Hinden, 23 November 1950; cf. Box 87, File 2, fo. 8–11, Stevens to Hinden, 13 March 1952; also correspondence with Hinden and Nicholson in FCB 6/6, fo. 184ff. Siaka Stevens, "Trade unionism in Sierra Leone", *Empire*, Vol. 11, No. 3, September 1948, p. 5.
77. *F.C.B.* Box 86, File 1B, fo. 111–14, Stevens to Nicholson, 15 May 1948.
78. *F.C.B.* Box 86, File 2, fo. 194–7, Stevens to Hinden, 3 December 1949.
79. *Ibid.* fo. 199–201, Stevens to Hinden, 4 July 1950.

CHAPTER 4

1. T. L. Hodgkin, *Nationalism in Colonial Africa* (1956), p. 23.
2. CO 554/132/33726/5, Discussion with Stanley, 27–8 October 1943.
3. N. Azikiwe, *My Odyssey* (1970), pp. 281–2.
4. F.C.B. Box 81, File 2, ff. 838, Hyde-Clarke to Nicolson, 17 Nov. 1953.
5. Cf. Basil Davidson, *Africa in Modern History* (1978), pp. 147–9.
6. J. F. Ade Ajayi and Michael Crowder, *History of West Africa*, II (1974), esp. pp. 571–5 (by J. B. Webster).

7. This is well pointed out in Henry S. Wilson, *Origins of West African Nationalism* (1969), on p. 41 and by the perceptive choice of cover design.
8. Hailey, NAPD, pp. 6, 7.
9. Extracts in A. H. M. Kirk-Greene (ed) *The Principles of Native Administration in Nigeria* (1965), pp. 238–45.
10. A. Creech Jones, *Labour's Colonial Policy* (Fabian Society, 1947), p. 7.
11. Dennis Austin, *Politics in Ghana, 1946–1960* (1964), Chapter III. It is interesting to compare the official *Report on the First Elections to the Western House of Assembly: General Election, 1951* (Ibadan, 1952). Here no previous registration of voters took place, many seats were left unfilled in the primary elections, and party activity seems to have been really intense only in Awolowo's town of Ikenne.
12. A detailed study of the working of this tradition in the politics of a major state (which incidently shows how many colonial officials became sympathetic to commoner participation) is Jarle Simensen, "Commoners, Chiefs and Colonial Government; British Policy and Local Politics in Akim Abuakwa", Ph.D. thesis, University of Trondheim, 1975.
13. Austin, *Politics in Ghana*, pp. 65–6, 116–7.
14. *Ibid.*, p. 113; Simensen, "Akim Abuakwa", II. pp. 333–5 J. Dunn and A. F. Robertson, *Dependence and Opportunity: Political Change in Ahafo* (Cambridge 1977) pp. 316–20.
15. For an early eye-witness account of this process, Basil Davidson, *The Liberation of Guiné* (Harmondsworth, 1969); cf. his *Africa in Modern History* (1978), pp. 341–50).
16. K. Post and G. Jenkins, *The Price of Liberty: Personality and politics in colonial Nigeria* (Cambridge, 1973), pp. 168–70; cf pp. 56–8 for earlier opposition to cutting-out by the Maiyegun League.
17. Gavin Williams, *Nigeria: Economy and Society* (1976), pp. 27, 208, 143.
18. See above pp. 63–4.
19. *Reports of the Commissioners of Enquiry into the Conduct of Certain Chiefs* (Freetown, 1957), 67, Report by Sir David Edwards on Bai Bairoh 29 January 1957.
20. *Ibid.*, pp. 23–8, Report on Bai Sebora Kamal II.
21. *Sierra Leone: Report of Commission of Inquiry into Disturbances in the Provinces* (Crown Agents, 1956), Chap. II (Cox Report).
22. Cf. *Report of the Commissioner of Inquiry into the Strikes and Riots in Freetown, Sierra Leone, during February 1955* (Freetown, 1955).
23. Cox Report, pp. 66, 17, 13.
24. Jacques Lombard, *Autorités traditionelles et pouvoirs européens en Afrique noire* (Paris, 1967), p. 11.
25. J. Suret-Canale, "La fin de la chefferie en Guinée", *Journal of African History* VII, 1966, pp. 459–93.
26. See the important study of R. A. Joseph. *Radical Nationalism in Cameroun* (Oxford 1977), esp. pp. 239–43, 298–300, 342–5.
27. D. Cruise O'Brien, in J. Dunn (ed) *West African States: Failure and Promise* (Cambridge 1978), p. 186.
28. Adrian Adams, *Le long voyage des gens du fleuve* (Paris, 1977). Dr Adams's work in "Jamaané" continues, executing the commitment implicit in the last paragraph of her book.
29. Basil Davidson, *Africa in Modern History* (1978).

CHAPTER 5

1. Colonial No 248, Gold Coast; Report by the Committee on Constitutional Reform, 1949, Para. 27. For the basis on which the conclusion quoted was reached see Author's Preface to M. Wight, *The Gold Coast Legislative Council* (1947).
2. Cmnd 6270 of 1975, *Overseas Development: the Changing Emphasis in British Aid Policies*, p. 21.
3. CO 847/36/47328, Unsigned memo on "Education Policy in Africa", May 1947.
4. Creech Jones to Stevenson, 197, 16 Aug. 1947, in Sessional Paper 5 of 1947, *Higher Education in the British West African Colonies* (Freetown 1947). *Report of the Sierra Leone Education Commission* (Freetown, 1954). I have also used papers in my own possession prepared for the visit of this Commission.
5. I recorded some impressions from a lecture tour in West Africa undertaken immediately afterwards in "Pan-Africanism after Rhodesia", *The World Today*, February 1966.

CHAPTER 6

1. *Proceedings of University of Ibadan Commission of Inquiry* (Ministry of Information, Lagos, 1971) Day 2, 15 February 1971, p. 53, " . . . one would be tempted to think in terms of the University structure itself which is sub-colonial. We inherited a lot of things, I am talking now in terms of facilities. It is a residential University. . . ."
2. *Parliamentary Papers* 1944–45, Vol. IV. [Asquith] *Report . . . on higher education in the colonies* (Cmd. 6647, 1944); Vol. V. [Elliot] *Report . . . on higher education in West Africa* (Cmd. 6655, 1945).
3. Eric Ashby, with Mary Anderson, *Universities: British, Indian, African* (London, 1966)—a masterly work on which this paper heavily relies.
4. Both reports are printed as appendices to Ashby, *Universities*.
5. Ashby, *Universities*, pp. 495, 211f.
6. Elliot *Report*, p. 18.
7. See the quotation from D. L. Balme, Ashby, *Universities*, p. 241.
8. Ashby, *Universities*, pp. 231ff.
9. J. T. Saunders, *University College Ibadan* (Cambridge, 1960), p. 167.
10. On "Quality" and "Standards" see Ashby, *Universities*, pp. 236ff, 259ff.
11. For Yaba, see O. Awolowo, *Awo* (Cambridge, 1960), pp. 115–16; Ashby, *Universities*, pp. 196–97. See also F. O. Ogunlade, "Yaba Higher College and the Formation of an Intellectual Elite" Ibadan MA thesis (1970).
12. This aspect is emphasized in A. Fajana, "The Controversy on Higher Education in Nigeria in the 1930s and 1940s", an unpublished paper read to the 16th Congress of the Historical Society of Nigeria, 1970. Dr. Fajana further argues that local colonial officials opposed university development out of fear for their own jobs.
13. K. Mellanby, *The Birth of Nigeria's University* (London, 1958), p. 77.
14. W. Moberly, *The Crisis in the University* (London, 1949), p. 218.

15. Mellanby, *Birth of Nigera's University*, pp. 155-6, 236; Saunders, *University College Ibadan*, p. 84.
16. Elliot *Report*, p. 57; by 1978, this trend appeared to have been reversed.
17. Elliot *Report*, p. 55.
18. Ashby, *Universities*, p. 244.
19. Saunders, p. 123; Mellanby, *Birth of Nigeria's University*, pp. 116-19.
20. Lockwood to Ashby, 1963—Ashby, *Universities*, pp. 286-7.
21. *Investment in Education*, (Report of the Commission on Post-School Certificate and Higher Education in Nigeria, Lagos, 1966), p. 22.
22. Mellanby, *Birth of Nigeria's University*, pp. 153ff.
23. Saunders, *University College Ibadan*, p. 165.
24. E.g. Leonard Barnes, *Africa in Eclipse* (London, 1971).
25. Mellanby, *Birth of Nigeria's University*, p. 103. See also p. 12.
26. *West Africa*, 22 February 1969, p. 223.

CHAPTER 7

1. Lothian Papers, Scottish Record Office, G.D.40/17/246, Oldham to Curtis, 8 January 1931, quoting Day.
2. G.D.40/17/234, Kerr to Coupland, 6 November 1929.
3. G.D.40/17/245, Kerr to Smuts, 13 February 1930, and enclosure.
4. G.D.40/17/247, Lothian to Day, 20 March, 1931.
5. G.D.40/17/234, Coupland to Kerr, 11 November, 1929.
6. G.D.40/17/248, Grigg to Lothian 22 July, 1930: G.D.40/17/257, Grigg to Lothian, 9, 14 September, 1931.
7. G.D.40/17/257, Lothian to Grigg, 11 September, 1930.
8. G.D.40/17/241, Jones to Kerr, 10 June, 1929.
9. *Ibid.*, Jones to Kerr, 24 February 1930.
10. G.D.40/17/259, Oldham to Lothian, 17, 21 September, 1931.
11. G.D.40/17/248, Flexner to Lothian, 20 June, 1930.
12. G.D.40/17/248, Lothian to Grigg, 14 July, 1930: Lothian to Harris, 17 September, 1930.
13. G.D.40/17/246, Lothian to C. H. Siepmann, 14 November, 1930.
14. G.D.40/17/247, Oldham to Curtis, 8 January, 1931, quoting Day.
15. G.D.40/17/243, Oldham to Kerr, 6 February, 1930, enclosing memo by Malinowski.
16. G.D.40/17/256, Curtis to Lothian, 10 July 1931, enclosing F. P. Keppel to Curtis, 30 June.

Index

Additional Abbreviations
AEF   *Afrique Equatoriale française*
CS   Civil Service
Col. Sec. Colonial Secretary
GC   Gold Coast
Gov.   Governor
MLC   Member of Legislative Council
NCBWA   National Congress of British West Africa
UCI   University College, Ibadan
PM   Prime Minister
S of S   Secretary of State
SL   Sierra Leone
US   Under-Secretary (AUS – Assistant Under-Secretary: DUS – Deputy Under-Secretary)
WA   West Africa

Aberdeen, University of, 94, 108, 110, 130n60
Aborigines Rights Protection Society (GC), 9
Accra municipality, 31
  riots of 1948, 6, 17, 19, 20, *43*, 67
Action Group (Nigeria), 46
Adams, Adrian (b. 1945), anthropologist, 82, 131n28
Adams, Sir Theodore S. (1885–1961), Malayan CS 1908–37, Chief Commissioner N. Nigeria, 1937–43, 37
Addison, Paul (b. 1943), historian, 40
Adelabu, G. Adegoke (1914–58), Nigerian politician, 77–8
African Studies Association (UK), 94, 112, 122
Agbekoya, movement of Nigerian farmers, 78
Aggrey, James E. Kwegyir (1875–1927), GC educationalist, 91

Agona (GC), 76
Ahafo, (GC), 76
Ajayi, Jacob F. Ade (b. 1929), historian, 49, 72
Akim Abuakwa (GC), 31, 76, 121n12
Algeria, 7, 10, 21–3
All Peoples' Congress (SL), 80
Amin, Idi (b. 1925), President of Uganda since 1971, 96
Arden–Clarke, Sir Charles N. (1898–1962), Gov. GC, 1949–57, 20–1, 45, 71
Asante, 31–2, 35–6, 72, 75–6
Ashby, Eric, (Baron) (b. 1904), botanist and educationalist, 100, 106, 108
Asquith, Cyril (1st Baron), (1890–1954), Chairman, Commission on Higher Education in the Colonies 1943–4, 99, 102–3, 107–8
Atlantic Charter, 15, 28
Attlee, Clement R. (1883–1967), 40

Index

Austin, Dennis (b. 1922), political scientist, 75–6
Avuncularism, 93–5, 122
Awolowo, Obafemi, (b. 1909) founder, Action Group, 19, 46, 131n11
Ayandele, Emmanuel A. (b. 1936), historian, 4
Ayew, John, farmers' leader in GC, 76
Azikiwe, Benjamin Nnamdi (b. 1904) founder NCNC, President of Nigeria 1960–6, 7, 19, 46, 48, 78 Governor Hodson, 4, 71–2

Bakel, (Senegal), 82
Baldwin, Stanley (1867–1947), 71, 121
Bamileke people (Cameroun), 81
Bassa people (Cameroun), 81
Beresford-Stooke, Sir George (b. 1897), Gov. SL 1948–53, 47, 64
Bevin, Ernest (1881–1951), 40
Blood, Sir Hilary R. R. (1893–1967), Col. Sec. SL 1934–42, The Gambia, 1942–7, 35, 55–6, 58
Blyden, Edward Wilmot (1832–1912), Afro-American writer, 92, 100
Blyden, Edward Wilmot III, scholar and politician, 92
Bo (SL), 55
Bonn, Moritz, J., 3
Bonthe (SL), 55–6
Boston, J. Fowell, SL Lawyer, MLC, 62
Bourdillon, Sir Bernard Henry (1883–1948), Indian CS 1908, Gov. Uganda 1932–35, Nigeria 1935–43, 30, 35, 37, 46
Brazzaville, Conference (1944), 5, 14, 18, 21, 51
Bright, Dr H. C. Bankole, (1883–1958), Creole politician, founder NCBWA, MLC 1924–39, 1951–7, 53, 64
Buell, Raymond L. (1896–1946), American student of international politics, 120
Burns, Sir Alan C. (b. 1887), Gov. British Honduras 1934–40, AUS CO 1940–1, Gov. GC 1941–7, 17, 28–32, 35–6, 39, 43, 60, 124–5n8, 11, 14, 18

Caine, Sir Sidney (b. 1902), AUS CO, 1944–47, DUS 1947–8, Director LSE 1957–67, 42
Cameroun, 7, 12, 18, 20–1, 81–2
Caradon, *see* Foot
Carnegie Corporation, 121
CAST Colleges, 90, 107
Central Africa, 4, 23; *see also* Rhodesia
Ceylon, 3
Channon, Harold J. (b. 1897), Professor of Biochemistry, University of Liverpool 1932–43, Member, Elliot Commission, 106
Chatham House, 15, 121
China, 100–1
Churchill, Sir Winston L. S. (1874–1965), xii, 15–16, 28, 51
Clifford, Sir Hugh C. (1866–1941), Malayan CS, Gov. GC 1912–19, Nigeria 1919–25, Ceylon 1925–7, Malaya 1927–9, 4
Cocoa, 11, 17, 26, 39, 81
 farmers 10, 43–4, 74–6, 78
Cohen, Sir Andrew B. (1909–68), Assistant Secretary, CO 1943–47, AUS 1947–51, Gov. Uganda, 1952–7, 21, 42–3
Colonial Development and Welfare Act, (1940), 15, 24, 58–60
 (1945), 17, 41, 64
Colonial Office, 4, 14–21, 24–46, 54–68, 90, 101–6
 Advisory Committee on Education, 14, 40–1, 59–60
 African Governors' Conferences (1947), 42
Commonwealth, 19, 23, 24, 26, 104, 117
 Ghana and, 45, 48, 83
Communism, 12, 13, 17, 55, 72
 and Cold War, 20, 43–5, 73
 in France, 5, 21, 82
Compagnie française de l'Afrique occidentale, 11
Congo, 95
Conrad, Joseph, (1857–1924), novelist, 110
Conservative and Unionist Party (UK), 23

Index

Conton, William F. (b. 1925), SL writer and educationalist, 91
Convention Peoples' Party (Ghana), 6–7, 21, 45, 74–6
Conway, H. E., 65
Coupland, Sir Reginald (1884–1952), historian, 119
Coussey, Sir James Henley (d. 1958), Ghanian jurist, Chairman, Committee on Constitutional Reform 1949, 6, 21, 44–5, 90
Cranborne, Viscount, (Robert A. J. Gascoyne Cecil, 5th Marquis of Salisbury, 1947), (1893–1972), S of S for Colonies 1942, 30, 40, 59
Creasy, Sir Gerald H. (b. 1897), CO 1920–47, Gov. GC, 1947–9, Malta, 1949–54, 43
Creoles, 38, 47, 52–66, 68, 78–9
Cripps, Sir R. Stafford (1889–1952), Labour MP and Minister 1930–50, 17
Currie, Sir James (1868–1937), Director of Education, Sudan 1900–14, 101
Curtis, Lionel G. (1872–1955), Imperial idealist, 14, 117–19
Czechoslovakia, 20, 43

Dahomey, 10
Dakar, 4, 82
Danquah, Joseph K. K. Boakye (1893–1965), Ghanaian politician, 19, 31–2, 35–6
Davidson, Basil R. (b. 1914), historian, 84
Dawe, Sir Arthur J. (1891–1950), Secretary to Commission on Freetown Municipality, 1926, AUS, CO 1938–45, DUS, 1945–7, 32, 54
Decker, Thomas A. L. (b. 1916), SL writer, 63
Delafosse, E. F. Maurice (1870–1926), administrator and scholar, 14
Depression of 1930s, 11, 15, 25
Diagne, Blaise (1872–1934), Senegalese Deputy 1914–34, 10
Diamonds, 47, 66, 79
Dougall, James W. C. (b. 1896) Scottish missionary, Principal Jeanes School Kabete, Kenya, 1925, 31, 120
Duff, James F. (1898–1970), Warden of the Durham Colleges, 1937–60, Member Elliot Commission, 101
Durham, University of, 9, 100–1, 108

East Africa, 4, 23, 34–6, 39–40, 120; *see also* Kenya
Eboué, A. Félix S. (1884–1944), Guyanese, Governor-General, AEF 1940–44, 18
Education, 33, 59–60, 64–5, Part II *passim*
Elliot, Walter E. (1888–1958), Cons. M.P. and Minister, Chairman, Commission on Higher Education in West Africa, 18, 33, 41–3, 60, 85, 97, 99–111, 126n54
Enugu, 44
Ethiopia, 12
Examinations, 94–5, 104, 109
Executive Council, appointment of Africans, 29–30, 34–6, 45, 60–1, 92
Extra-mural education, 6, 42, 64, 92

Fabian Colonial Bureau, 40–1, 65–8, 71, 89, 96
Fage, John D. (b. 1921), historian, x, 112
Fanon, Frantz (1925–6), Martiniquais psychiatrist and revolutionary, 7–8
FIDES, 17
Fisher, Herbert A. L. (1865–1940), historian and Liberal politician, 119
Foot, Hugh M. (Baron Caradon) (b. 1907), Chief Sec Nigeria, 1947–51, Gov Jamaica, 1951–7, Cyprus 1957–60, British Minister at UN, 1964–70, 7, 19, 44–6, 64, 130n60
Fourah Bay College, 53, 60, 89–93, 100–1, 111
France, African policies, 4–6, 9–10, 12–14, 21–3, 50–1, 69, 80–4
French Union, 5, 19

France, African policies (*continued*)
 Popular Front government of 1936, 5, 14, 51
Freetown, 52–63, 80, 101
 City Council, 38, 53–4, 58, 61–3
Fry, E. Maxwell (b. 1899) architect, Town Planning Adviser, West Africa, 1943–5, 32, 105
Fyfe, Christopher (b. 1919), historian, 93

Gambia, xii, 35, 38, 96
 small size, 38, 46–7, 52
Garvey, Marcus M. (1887–1940), charismatic Jamaican, 12
de Gaulle, Charles (1890–1970), 5, 18, 23, 81
Germany, 12, *see* National Socialism
Ghana, 9, 11, 20–1, 26, *29–32*, *35–6*, *42–6*, 59–61; *see* Accra Riots, Convention Peoples' Party
Gilbert, Leslie H. (b. 1892), teacher of history, 89
Gold Coast, *see* Ghana
Gowon, Yakubu (b. 1934), Head of Nigerian State 1966–7, 8
Greene, Graham (b. 1904), novelist, 54
Grigg, Edward W. M. (1st Baron Altrincham) (1879–1955), Kenya 1925–31, Liberal MP, 1922–25, Cons. MP and Minister 1933–45, 119–20
Gueye, Laminè (1891–1968), Senegalese politician, 5
Guggisberg, Sir Frederick S. (1869–1930), Gov. GC, 1919–27, 11
Guiné-Bissao, 8, 77
Guinea, 7, 20, 81
Gulama, Julius (d. 1952), Chief of Kaiyamba, SL, 78

Hailey, William Malcolm, 1st Baron (1872–1969), Indian CS 1895–1934, 15–16, *27–31*, *34–5*, 37, 40, 46, 72
 African Survey 15, 121
 visits Freetown 1940, 57–8
Hall, George H. 1st Viscount (1881–1965), Parliamentary US at CO, 1940–2, S of S 1945–6, 40
Hall, Sir Noel F. (b. 1902), Development Adviser, West Africa, 1943–5, 32
Harlech, *see* Ormsby-Gore
Harris, William Wade (c. 1865–1929), Grebo prophet, 72
Hayford, J. E. Casely (1866–1930), GC politician, founder NCBWA, 72
Healey, Dennis W. (b. 1917), Sec. International Dept. Labour Party, 1945–52, Labour MP and Minister since 1952, 66
Hinden, Rita (1908–71), Fabian Socialist, 66–7
Hitler, Adolf (1889–1945), ix, 12
Hobson, John A. (1858–1940), economist, 14
Hodgkin, Thomas L. (b. 1910), historian, Palestine CS 1934–36, Secretary Oxford University Delegacy for Extra-mural studies 1945–52, 42, 70, 72, 83, 92, 116
Hodson, Sir Arnold W. (1881–1944), Gov. SL 1930–34, GC, 1934–41, 4, 71
Hopkins, Anthony G. historian, 11
Houphouet-Boigny, Felix (b. 1905), Deputy and Minister in French Governments 1945–58, President, Ivory Coast since 1958, 5, 19, 21, 82–4

Ibadan, 77–8
 University, 90, 96, 99, 103, 105, 108–10
Ife University, 106, 109
Igbo people, 46, 72
Income-tax, 30, 59
India, 3, 10, 13, 16, 43, 50
 experience applied to Africa, 28, 35, 44, 84, 104, 127n62
Indochina, 10, 17, 21
International African Institute, 121
Ivory Coast, 7, 17, 21, 82–3

Jaja (c. 1821–91), founder of Opobo, invoked by Wallace-Johnson, 55
Japan, 10, 12

Index

Jardine, Sir Douglas J. (1888–1946), Gov SL, 1937–41, 53–9, 62
Jones, Arthur Creech (1891–1964), Parity US for Colonies 1945–6, S of S 1946–50, 14, 17–18, *40–1*, 45, 62–3, 74
  Vice Chairman Elliot Commission, 126n54
Jones, Thomas Jesse (1873–1914), Director Phelps-Stokes Fund 1913–46, 120

Kamara, Peter, Temne leader, 80
Kaniki, Dr Martin, historian, 53
Kenya, 4, 10, 21, 23, 119
Kenyatta, Jomo (1891–1978), President of Kenya 1962–78, 12
Kerr, Philip H., Marquess of Lothian (1882–1940), Sec. Rhodes Trust and Liberal politician, 14, *117–21*
Korean war 1950–3, 46
Kouyaté, Tiémoho Garan (d. c. 1942), Malian radical, 12
Kumasi, 31, 36, 43

Labour Party (UK), 13, 40–2, 65–7, 89
Lagos, 37
  Strike of 1945, 44–5
Lambo, Thomas Adeoye (b. 1923), Psychiatrist, Vice-Chancellor University of Ibadan, 1968–71, 99, 105, 110, 132n1
League of Nations, 11
Lenin, V. I. (1870–1924), 72
Leys, Norman M. (1875–), critic of colonialism in Kenya, 120
Lipton, Michael, economist, 84
Little, Kenneth L. (b. 1908), anthropologist, 65
Local government, 18, 28, 30–1, 42, 58, 74–5, 79; *see* Freetown municipality
London School of Economics, 3, 4, 5, 117
London University, 94, 104, 108–9
Lothian, *see* Kerr
Low, D. Anthony (b. 1927), historian, 41–2
Lugard, Frderick J. D., 1st Baron (1855–1945), 11, 25, 29

Lunsar, (SL), 55
Lyttleton, Oliver (1st Viscount Chandos) (1893–1972), Cons. MP 1940–54, S of S for Colonies 1951–4, 21

Macdonald, Malcolm J. (b. 1901), S of S for Colonies 1935, 1938–40, Gov-General Malaya, 1946–8, Kenya 1963–4, 3–4, 13, 15, 51
Macmillan, Harold (b. 1894), ix, 8, 23, 46
Macmillan, William M. (1885–1974), historian, 55–6
Makeni, (SL), 79
Malaya, 20–1, 28, 43, 89
Malinowski, Bronislaw (1884–1942), anthropologist, 121
Manchester, University of, 89, 112–14
Mano (SL), 55
Mao Tse-tung (1893–1976), 43
Marampa, (SL), 56, 66
Margai, Sir Milton A. S. (1895–1964), physician, founder SLPP, PM SL 1954–64, 79
Marx, Karl (1818–83), 16, 50, 72
Medical services, 30
  education, 93, 106–7
Mellanby, Sir Kenneth (b. 1905), Principal University College, Ibadan, 1947–53, 105, 110
Mikardo, Ian (b. 1908), Labour MP 1945–59 and since 1964, 41
Milner, Alfred, 1st Viscount (1854–1925), Imperialist, 14, 117
Mining industry, 7, 10, 54–6, 66–7
Mitterand, François M. M. (b. 1916), Minister for Overseas Territories 1950–1, 82
Moberly, Sir Walter H. (1881–1974), Chairman University Grants Committee 1935–49, 103
Modu, Alikali, III, Chief of Maforki (Port Loko) SL, 1949–57, 79–80
Montgomery, Bernard L. (Viscount) (1887–1976), CIGS 1946–8, 44
Morel, Edmund D. (1873–1924), founder of Union of Democratic Control, 14

Index

Morrison, Herbert S. (1885–1965), 40
Moutet, Marius, French Socialist, 14
Moyamba (SL), 55, 63
Moyne (Guinness, Walter E. 1st Baron) (1880–1944), Chairman West Indies Royal Commission 1938–9, S of S for Colonies 1941–2, 12, 28–30, 32, 40

Namier, Sir Lewis B. (1888–1960), historian, 45, 91–2, 113
National Congress of British West Africa, 4, 53
National Council of Nigeria and the Cameroons, 46, 78
National Council of Sierra Leone, 47
National Socialism, 56
Native Authorities, 25–8, 74
  in GC, 31–2, 34–7
  in SL, 58–9, 63, 67–8
Nigeria, 7, 26, 29–30, 61, 74, 77–8, 84–5, 90
  constitutional change, 19, 36–8, 44–6
  civil war, 7–8, 46, 94, 96
  universities, 105–10
Nikoe, Ashie, GC farmers' leader, 76
Nisbet, H. A., Labour Secretary, SL, 57, 65
Njala (SL), 93
Njoko, Eni (1918–74) Nigerian botanist, Minister of Mines 1952–3, 89
Nkrumah, Kwame (c. 1909–72), 6–7, 20–1, 43–5, 48, 71, 82–3
Northern Peoples' Congress (Nigeria), 46, 78

Ofori Atta I (1881–1943), Paramount Chief of Akim Abuakwa 1912–43, 31–2, 35
Oldham, Joseph H. (1874–1969), Christian activist, 120
Oliver, Roland A. (b. 1923), historian, x, 112
Onoge, O, Nigerian sociologist, 99, 110
Orde-Browne, Sir Granville St. J (1883–1947), Labour Adviser to CO 1938–47, 65

Ormsby-Gore, William G. A. (4th Baron Harlech) (1885–1964), Parliamentary US for Colonies 1922–4, 1924–9, S of S 1936–8, 33
Oxford University, 105, 117–21

Padmore, George (M.I.M. Nurse) (1902–59), Trinidadian pan-African, 9, 12, 53
PAIGC, 8, 84
Parliament, 3–4, 13, 16, 41, 56
  Committee of 1865, 6, 9, 24, 52
Parry, Edgar (b. 1904), Labour officer and Commissioner SL 1942–8, Asst. Labour Adviser to CO, 1948–54, Deputy 1954–61, 42, 65–9, 72
Parti Democratique de Guineé, 51
Partnership, 16, 39
Peoples' Educational Association, SL, 92
  GC, 74
Pepel, SL, 55, 66
Perham, Dame Margery (b. 1895), pioneer Africanist, 112, 119–20
Pleven, René J. (b. 1901), Minister of Colonies, 1944, PM 1950–2, 82
Porter, Arthur T. (b. 1924), historian, 91, 93
Port Loko, SL, 79–80
Pujehun, SL, 92

Radcliffe-Brown, A. R. (1881–1955), anthropologist, 120
Ranger, Terence O., historian, x
Rassemblement Democratique African, 82
Rhodesia, 4, 95–6
Rhodes Trust, 14, 117–21
Richards, Arthur F., 1st Baron Milverton (1885–78), Malayan CS 1908–30, Gov, The Gambia 1933–6, Nigeria 1943–7, 17, 19, 37–9, 45
Robinson, Kenneth E. (b. 1914), historian, Asst. Sec. CO, 1946–8, 51
Robinson, Ronald E. (b. 1920), historian, Research Officer, CO 1947–9, x–xi, 42
Robson, William A. (b. 1895) Professor of Public Administration, LSE, 63

Index

Rockefeller Foundation, 118, 121
Round Table, 14, 117
Ruskin College, 67

Sarraut, Albert M. (1872–1962), French politician, 11
Sartre, Jean-Paul (b. 1905), writer, 8
Saunders, John T. (1888–1965), Principal University College Ibadan 1953–6, 103, 105
Senegal, 5, 7, 9, 10, 82
Senghor, Léopold Sédar (b. 1906), President of Senegal since 1958, 5, 82
Sierra Leone, 6, 22, 25–6, 38, 42, 46–7, 51–69; see also Fourah Bay College
Peoples' Party, 47, 64, 78–80
Organization Society, 63
Sierra Leone Studies, 93
Sissoko, Fily Dabo, Deputy, 5
Smuts, Jan C. (1870–1950), South African PM, 14, 40, 118, 120
South Africa, 4, 8, 12, 23, 41, 44, 117; see also Smuts
Stanley, Oliver F. G. (1896–1950), S of S for Colonies, 1942–5, 32–8, 40, 61, 71, 101–2
Stevens, Siaka Probyn (b. 1905), PM SL 1968, President since 1971, 42, 66–8, 73, 91–2
Stevenson, Sir Hubert C. (b. 1888), Gov SL, 1941–8, 38, 60–1
Swayne, Anthony C. (b. 1913), colonial servant, 61–2
Swinton, (Philip Cunliffe-Lister, 1st Earl of) (1884–1972), S of S for Colonies 1931–5, Resident Minister in West Africa, 1942–4, 32–3

Tass, Bai Farima II, Chief of Magbema SL 1945–57, Minister without portfolio 1951–7, 80
Taylor, Walter, extra-mural teacher, 92
Temne people (SL), 58, 79–80
Thuku, Harry (1895–1970), Kenyan political pioneer, 10
Togoland, 31, 75n
Toure, Ahmed Sekou (b. 1922), founder of RDA, 1947, President of Guinea since 1958, 20, 73, 81
Trade Unions, 18, 42, 56–7, 65–8, 72–3
West African Federation of (1945), 67
World Federation of, 67

Uganda, 23, 96
Union des Populations du Cameroun, 20, 81
Union of Soviet Socialist Republics, 10, 12, 13
United Africa Company, 11
United Gold Coast Convention, 43
United Nations, 48, 93
United States of America, 8, 16, 17, 28, 92
academic influence, 108, 110
Universities, 18, 33, 85, Part II passim; see also under individual universities

Wallace-Johnson, Isaac T. A. (1895–1945), SL journalist, 12, 54–7, 66–7, 72–3
War, First World, 10
Second World, xi, 6, 15–16, 27–38, 51
Watson, A. Aiken (1897–1969), Lawyer, Chairman Gold Coast Commission 1948, 44–5, 71
Wedgwood, Josiah Clement, 1st Baron, (1872–1943), Liberal, later Labour MP, 1906–42, 12, 120
West Africa, 53
West African Youth League, 54–7, 65, 69
Wight, R. J. Martin (1913–72), historian, 6, 90
Williams, O. G. R. (1886–1954), Assistant Secretary, CO, 1926–46, 32–5, 38, 42, 44, 52–60
Willink, Sir Henry U. (1894–1973), Minister of Health 1943–5, Master of Magdalene College, Cambridge 1948–66, 46
Wilson, T. Woodrow, (1856–1924), 10
Wright, Claudius E. barrister, MLC SL, 53

Yaba Higher College, 104, 106, 132n12
Yoruba people, 46, 72, 77–8

WITHDRAWN